THE CHRISTIAN ETHOS

A. TROOST

PAIDEIA
PRESS

www.paideiapress.ca

The Christian Ethos — A Philosophical Survey

A publication of Paideia Press (3248 Twenty First St., Jordan Station, Ontario, Canada L0R 1S0).

First published 1983
by Patmos
4 Aucamp Street
9301 Bloemfontein
South Africa

Translated by Kobus and Yvonne Smit, Bloemfontein

Edited by Don Sedgwick, Toronto

ISBN 978-0-88815-327-2

CONTENTS

About the Author

PROFESSOR ANDREE TROOST (1916-2008) began his professional career as a minister. He served consecutively in the congregations of Vleuten De Meern (five years), Beetgum (four years), Kootwijk (three years) and Rotterdam, where he was minister to the student congregation for five years. While at Kootwijk he graduated as Doctor of Theology on a thesis "Casuistry and Situation Ethics" in 1958. He started his academic career as extraordinary professor in social ethics in the Faculty of Economics of the Free University of Amsterdam during 1964. The following year he also lectured in the Faculty of Social Sciences. In 1967 he became a full professor in Social Ethics in the Faculty of Economic Sciences, the Sub-Faculties of Social and Cultural Sciences, Pedagogics and Andragology, as well as in the Central Interfaculty for Philosophy.

Professor Troost was a popular lecturer and was invited by universities from various countries to be a visiting professor. He was co-editor of the periodical *Philosophia Reformata*, the forum for writings about the Philosophy of the Cosmonomic Idea, as well as the international periodical *Forum*.

Preface

THE CHRISTIAN ETHOS is a collection of related articles from several different sources. Some of the chapters have been translated from my earlier book, *Geen aardse macht begeren wij (We Desire No Earthly Power)*, published by Buijten & Schipperheijn in Amsterdam in 1976. Other chapters are revisions of my lectures delivered at the Central Interfaculty of the Free University of Amsterdam and those given as a lecturer at the Reformed Theological College in Geelong, Australia. A lecture delivered at the University of the Orange Free State, Bloemfontein, South Africa in 1975 is also included. As a whole, *The Christian Ethos* is essentially a popular and preliminary approach to a systematic study of philosophical ethics.

In gratitude I dedicate this volume to the staff of the Reformed Theological College at Geelong, who invited me in 1979 to lecture for a period of seven weeks on the subject of philosophical ethics. Most of the present chapters constitute the material I presented at that time.

To Professor J.H. Smit I wish to express my thanks for his trouble, and that of his collaborators, to publish this work in English. Professor Smit served as a very willing and capable editor for this publication.

Professor A. Troost
FREE UNIVERSITY
AMSTERDAM
1983

CHAPTER 1

Ethics: In Philosophy, Theology and Everyday Life

Current View of Ethics

FOR THE MOMENT, we shall begin by adopting the current idea that ethics is the science dealing with conduct. This study of good or bad actions involves a large complex of questions, including that of norms and values. Ethics always concerns itself with an explanation of human actions. It questions what is implied by human conduct, ways of differentiation, arguments, and our motivations and goals. Ethics deals with the effects of our conduct both on an individual and a societal level.

When we consider these aspects of ethics, we are immediately faced with some preliminary questions. Since ancient times such a discussion has been summarised in the so-called *"prolegomena,"* i.e., the things that must be said first. The answers to these first questions determine to a large extent the actual problems of ethics. One of the first problems to be

9

discussed is the nature of ethics itself.

In his *"Einfuhrung in die Ethik,"* H.H. Schrey sees ethics as the theory of the motivations for human actions. Many other philosophers have recently adopted a similar view. I have very little objection to labelling ethics as motivation-theory. The crucial issue is our philosophical view of reality and our view of what is active in our motivations. When we see and believe the divine creation-order as the continuing will and power of God the creator, sustaining everything He has created, then we can easily acknowledge how the structures of human life motivate our actions.

We are faced here with the relation of man to his actions. In order to understand this relation, it makes sense to distinguish clearly between the two. In terms of the encyclopedia of the sciences, philosophical anthropology is defined as the doctrine of man and humanity as a totality. Philosophical ethics, or, as it has often been called, praxiology, is quite different; it is the study of human actions or conduct in general. I do not mean to suggest a psychological theory of conduct. I merely intend a philosophical theory of the general structures of human conduct and actions, set against a background of philosophical anthropology as a whole.

Philosophy and Ethics

Even at this early stage we are faced with a problem: what determines the parameters of a field of study? The problem of defining and delineating the various sciences and their subdisciplines actually belongs to the sphere of science-theory. One of the tasks of the theory of science is to analyse the *criteria* for differentiating between the main sciences. Unfortunately, a generally accepted encyclopedia of the sciences does not exist.

In this history of Western science, philosophy often played the part of a "studium general." It fulfilled the purpose of general reflection, in contrast to the typical examinations of the special sciences. Within the realm of ancient philosophy, many questions were discussed, including those of the natural sciences, for example. Until recently, faculties of mathematics and natural science still carried the official name of faculties of the philosophy of nature.

Gradually, however, sciences such as theology, pedagogics, sociology and psychology had developed so independently that a common misunderstanding arose. It is quite correct to say that all sciences severed themselves from the mother's womb of philosophy, in which they came to being, gradually developed, and in modern times started to lead an independent and "autonomous" life apart from philosophy.

It is incorrect, however, to suggest that this "mother" is now in her death throes. According to its nature, philosophy in the sense of implicit philosophical assumptions retains its leading role within the special sciences. Thus, for example, theoretical pedagogics is still called philosophical pedagogics.

Is Ethics both "Practical" and "Applied" Philosophy? The philosophers from Ancient Greece onward often answered this question affirmatively. Nevertheless, the issue is more complicated than it at first appears. A great deal depends on what is understood by science and what relation exists between knowledge in theory and knowledge in practice.

We must therefore derive our answer from the theory of knowledge in general and particularly from the theory of science. The latter subject is beyond the scope of our present discussion, but I will draw the following conclusion. Ethics is not applied philosophy, nor even a so-called "practical philosophy." Ethics is a *theme* of general philosophy – an extension of philosophical anthropology.

Cosmology, anthropology, philosophical sociology, and ethics, or praxiology, can be regarded as the main themes of general systematic philosophy. The most encompassing of these themes in this foundational philosophy is cosmology. Due to an old tradition this study is often called "ontology" or "general theory of being" (Greek: to on = the being).

In cosmology, philosophical attention is repeatedly directed to man as one of the many particular givens in the cosmos and to his relations with non-human creatures. Above all, attention is paid to his central position in the whole of the cosmos. This is the origin of a philosophical theory of man: anthropology. As a form of philosophy it is distinguished from biological, physiological, psychological and cultural anthropology.

A basic characteristic of philosophy is its integrating and total view, which surveys various aspects and their interwovenness. Philosophy surpasses all these aspects in a view of totality and of unity in the totality. And this takes place within the non-scientific perspective of a vital conviction about the origin and destination of man and the world.

No man is an isolated individual. It is characteristic of his basic situation that he is related to God and to his fellow men. The relation between God and man encompasses the whole of human life and could therefore be called "religion." Religion is not one area or sphere of life but is the service of God (or an idol) in every domain of human life.

Philosophical sociology is the study of these realms. It investigates types of societal forms (communal, institutional and associational). A great deal of human life involves these structures and relations. A human being nearly always acts within societal structures. Therefore, anthropology includes philosophical sociology, and both lead to praxiology. This praxiology (or philosophical ethics) concerns human praxis – practical life.

Because we are focusing here on the concept of ethics, I will not go into a detailed explanation of the three central religious relationships in which man lives. I must assume an understanding of these relationships: the relation between man and his own temporal life in its interwovenness with all the rest of the cosmic creatures; second, the relation between man and his fellow men; and third, the basic relation between man and God in which the two other relationships are rooted.

I will take a similar approach to the main features of philosophical sociology. Presupposed in the following discussion is a theory of societal structures that suggests each one is qualified by some or other cosmic aspect. I must also forego an explanation of the relationship between the spiritual body of Christ on the one hand and the spiritual unity of mankind in Adam on the other hand, and the spiritual antithesis between them. I will proceed by assuming a certain understanding of these matters.

A discussion of the nature of ethics often begins with what is known as a "nominal definition," based on current usage or popular opinion. From this readily understood starting point we can proceed to a more accurate, theoretical definition.

However, such a theoretical definition can only be understood if we know the presuppositions behind it. In our case we need to look at certain anthropological presuppositions. Before proceeding, therefore, I will offer a short anthropological outline.

a) There are four sub-structures in the human mode of existence (see figure A, p. 29), viz. the physical, organic, psychic and act-structure of the human body.

14

b) "Structures" are the law-side of reality.

c) The act-structure shows different depth layers:

   i) The inner acts themselves, which have an intentional character. Most of these are directed toward external deeds in which they are transposed. Every external deed is a result of internal decisions, habits, dispositions, and a particular mentality.

   ii) The acts are embedded in one's dispositions, habits and character and are rooted in an attitude or mentality.

   iii) Acts and dispositions are rooted in a basic attitude toward life, which we call the "ethos" (see figures B and C, p. 30).

The first part of the following definition should be viewed against the background of these philosophical presuppositions. (The second part can only be understood through cosmological insights which lie outside the scope of the present chapter.) I would therefore define philosophical ethics in the following way:

a) Philosophical ethics, also correctly called praxiology, is a specific theme of systematic philosophy. It primarily directs itself to the particular depth-dimension of the act-structure of human existence that we call the "ethos." This philosophical theme is thus re-

15

ferred to as "ethology." Philosophical ethics directs itself to the depth-dimension of the individual and social "dispositions" and "social structures." This dimension is founded in the ethos. As a result, philosophical ethics is secondarily the "theory of dispositions."

b) Both these themes must be viewed in a dual perspective: the origin and destination in the cosmic unfolding and converging dynamics; and the law-side and subject-side of human actions.

We can therefore say, very briefly, that praxiology is both ethology and the theory of dispositions. Of course, such a short definition can only be understood properly in the context in which it originated. In this case the context is the foundational themes of general philosophy.

In traditional ethics there is a great deal of ambiguity and uncertainty about the significance of such things as habits, customs, and societal structures. This uncertainty poses problems for our idea of norms. But in the definition I have given, all these elements find their natural place in the structure of human actions. Seen in the light of philosophical cosmology, the problem of "norms and values" is placed once again in the philosophical context in which it naturally arises. Moreover, the dynamics of life are emphasised by the second part of the definition.

A strictly isolated treatment of ethics is, in fact,

an impossibility. This is also true for other sciences. Every specialist must, to a certain extent, generalise. In philosophical ethics the totality of philosophy is present, although usually in a concealed form. The pre-scientific, practical, and religious premises are also present, mostly by implication.

I want to make a clear distinction here. Philosophical ethics is a philosophical theme; ethics is a special science. This is one of the practical reasons why I prefer to use different terms, namely, praxiology and ethics. The themes that have traditionally been treated in philosophical ethics and partly also in theological ethics should, in my opinion, be treated in praxiology.

As a science, praxiology has something in common with ethics as a special science: praxiology usually cannot give firm prescriptions for concrete practical life. Praxiology has this in common with all the sciences.

Except in the territory of the practice of science itself (i.e., the field of scientific investigations), science is never practice itself. The special sciences come closer to being practice than does philosophy. But praxiology has a more fundamental character and therefore more general and abstract qualities than the special sciences.

We turn now to the question of typical moral action. Are all kinds of human action "moral"? In reflecting on the typical nature and limits of ethics, philosophers have often made a common observation.

Neither an historical nor a strictly factual study would suggest that all kinds of human action should be studied in ethics. Today an indiscriminate definition of ethics as the "science of human actions," without any qualification, is hardly ever found. This is much too general language for a useful definition. A more precise delimination is necessary, especially if all kinds of typical actions are regarded as either "moral" or "immoral."

As a result, the definition is often expanded to say that ethics is the science of human actions from the point of view of good and evil, or of norms and values. But experience suggests that even this is too wide a field of study. In fact, norms and values, and questions of good and evil, should be and are, in fact, treated in various sciences. For example, economics deals with good and evil in an economical sense; theology treats good and evil in relation to the content of our faith, explaining the doctrine of Scriptures and rejecting any deviations from biblical teachings; and aesthetics deals with the problematics of harmony and disharmony, beauty and ugliness.

We must therefore look for an even more precise definition of praxiology. W. Banning, for example, says that ethics is concerned with human actions from the point of view of the *highest* good and evil. This view is certainly more in line with the oldest traditions in ethics.

My own perspective is related, but not identical, to this view. As we have seen, human actions are rooted in the human ethos, in a religious-ethical mentality. In that depth-dimension the various activities of human life are concentrated in the last or highest principles of life. These are expressed in witnesses and confessions of faith.

From this point of view we can understand the viewpoint of Banning. In our ethos we are directed to something that is the "highest." I would say we are directed to the central religious commandment of love; in the last analysis, this determines what is good or evil.

In traditional ethics (called philosophical ethics or theological ethics), sexuality and related issues in marriage, the life of children and society are all central. We also find discussions about the following issues: the nature of conscience, how it originates and functions; truth and deceit, at the sick bed, for example; and property and theft, sometimes in connection with tax returns, etc.

Of course, this is a very arbitrary selection of all the questions which can arise in the abundance of life. Why have these questions been the predominant subjects of ethics? Why are such acts called "typical" moral actions (even though this is basically a correct assumption)?

In theoretical textbooks, ethics is often introduced as the theory of moral actions. Here only a limited number of topics are treated.

Theological ethics in particular often treats these issues in the artificially enlarged cadre of the ten commandments.

The tradition mentioned in the preceding paragraphs, however, reflects a rather arbitrary treatment. There are many questions in human life concerning good and evil that are not treated in traditional ethics. At the same time, other issues are central, e.g., investigations about man's love-life in its different expressions and relationships, especially in connection with sexuality and procreation.

Ethics as a Special Science

The traditional idea of ethics appears to be rather uncertain, ambiguous, and arbitrary, and should therefore be repudiated. In all the above-mentioned subjects, real problems certainly exist. But the answers to these problems are to be found in a number of special sciences, not in philosophical ethics or praxiology.

The question of which science should deal with the matter depends on the character of the question. Is it related primarily to economics, theology, the juridical sciences, linguistics, sociology, aesthetics, or some other special science? As in many questions, perhaps more than one science is involved. If practical and scientific help is necessary on a particular issue of good and evil, we should first consult the special science or sciences that are directly related to the question at hand.

Among the special sciences we include ethics in the sense of a special science that deals with issues relating to man's love life. Love, in this special moral sense, is an aspect of life that cannot be identified with, nor reduced to, another. This irreducible moral aspect qualifies societal relations such as marriage, family and friendship. Each of these relations provides a specific or typical character to the love, qualifying the societal form in question.

Neighbourly love also functions in the typical inter-individual relations between men outside societal structures such as marriage, family and friendship. Examples of these structures include the areas of medical practice, social work, youth work, and care for the aged, displaced, refugees and children. Neighbourly love also functions in the incidental assistance given in emergencies, such as fires, car accidents and financial crises.

Within some of these relationships of a typical moral nature, sexuality becomes a very important question. I would like to *reserve ethics as a special science* for the study of neighbourly love in these typically moral relations. This is a traditional approach, in so far as these problems have always been treated by, and have often stood in, the centre of ethics, including philosophical and theological ethics. At the same time, my conception implies (within an encyclopedic understanding of the sciences) a delimitation of ethics as a special science distinct from philosophical ethics.

All the other questions, which are not typically qualified by the aspect of moral love, are qualified

21

by one of the other normative aspects of the human act-structure. As questions, they have to be assigned to these non-ethical aspects and to the special field of the sciences related to these other sectors of human life.

For this reason, Christians have an extremely important task – to develop Christian special sciences according to the nature of science. Such Christian sciences could replace the inexpert work of philosophers, theologians and ministers who often judge difficult and complicated questions. In fact, these should be treated by experts in the various special sciences.

In this connection, a final remark is due about the relation between praxiology and ethics as a special science. In spite of the common use of the term "ethics" for both these sciences, there is no *special* relation between the two. The relation is there without any doubt, but in principle it is the same as that between philosophical ethics and the other special sciences.

Praxiology relates to all the special sciences in a foundational way. Philosophy – including anthropology, sociology and praxiology as philosophical themes – is presupposed in the methods and thought patterns of all the special sciences.

Theological and Philosophical Ethics

Since the time of the Ancient Greek philosophers, Western philosophy has been inspired by the ideal of providing humanity with a scientific doctrine of life and with scientific guidance for life. Cicero, for example, called philosophy the "dux vitae," the rational guide to life. Later, Christian theologians adopted this idea, applying it to theology as the rational guide to life. In doing so they woefully identified their theology with the Word of God itself: theology, the guide to life! Is this correct? Perhaps we should discuss this question in the light of its history.

Christians had to struggle for the first three or four centuries with a number of political and spiritual enemies. These enemies came from both inside and outside their ranks. One of the practical problems for early Christians was how to live their daily life in a heathen world. We know from the letters of Paul to the Corinthians, Ephesians and Romans how difficult the practical life of Christians could be during this time.

But Paul did not answer the questions about whether it was permissible to be a soldier, to keep the Lord's Day (Rom. 14:5; Col. 2:16), or to be circumcised (Gal. 6:15). And there are many other questions he omitted or to which he did not give a decisive answer. But he did warn that we should not judge one another anymore (Rom. 14:13). He also fought against the Jewish enemies in the church because they wanted to impose a yoke of bondage on the believers (Gal. 5:1).

Nevertheless, in imitating philosophical ethics, the first theological ethics arose. The first writings on this subject were produced by Ambrosius, the great preacher of Milan. The title and even the content of his work entitled *Three Books on the Duties of the Clergyman* borrowed to a large extent from the pagan philosopher Cicero, and in particular his work *De Officiis* (On Duties).

On the other hand, many theologians refused to adopt any elements from philosophy. Tertullian, for example, was one of those who opposed this practice. He joined with those who wanted to see all philosophy replaced by theology, and philosophical ethics replaced by theological ethics.

At the same time, even *they* adopted the idea of ethics from the philosophers and from the Jewish tradition. For this reason, Christianity very soon degenerated into a moral system with an accompanying doctrine of the merit of good works.

As in the history of philosophy, so also in the history of theology a great deal of both sciences came to be called "practical." Theological ethics became an imitation of philosophical ethics with the same pretension to be the rational guide to life.

Teachers of theological ethics initially made this claim as a substitute for philosophical ethics. Later, in the Middle Ages, they advanced its claims as a supernatural addition or complement to natural ethics. They thought a super-natural complement was needed to fill up what was lacking in natural ethics. Hence, they proposed a theological ethics with, in its centre, the three virtues of faith, hope and love. Natural ethics was said to be philosophical in nature;

in its centre were the four old Platonic virtues of bravery, moderation, wisdom, and righteousness.

At the time of the Reformation, the Reformers did not immediately develop an ethic. In a very practical way, they certainly explained the ten commandments and tried to apply these commandments to daily life in the way that we find, for example, in the Heidelberg Catechism. But a systematically developed ethics, following dogmatics, did not develop until later in the 17th century (e.g., Daneus, Admesius).

As far as I can determine, this form of ethics was a degeneration of Reformational theology into post-Reformational, rationalistic orthodoxy. Theological ethics attempted to cover the whole of life with a network of prescriptions, commandments, and prohibitions.

The same development occurred at this time in the Roman Catholic Church. It was the era of the great and famous moral systems of the Jesuits. They combined natural philosophical ethics with theological ethics according to the medieval life-view of the two realms: nature and supernature, church and world, reason and faith, natural general revelation and special revelation, science and the Scriptures, worldly life and spiritual life, nature and grace.

This dualistic view of life was altered in principle by the Reformation. Yet several centuries passed before a Reformational view of the unity of life could break through into scientific thought. I am referring primarily to the way in which the unity of

God's Word in Christ, in creation and redemption, inspired philosophical thinking.

In the meantime, the gap between natural life and spiritual life in Protestant theological thinking had become more and more identified with the gap in humanistic thinking between nature and freedom. This identification was unmasked and exposed by the breakthrough of the Reformational principle of the unity of life. Philosophers identified a very strong influence of non-Christian, nonbiblical thinking upon both theology and Christian practical life.

Conclusion

I would like to conclude this chapter with some remarks from a doctoral thesis on philosophy and the Scriptures submitted by Dr. Van der Stelt of Dordt College, U.S.A. in 1981. He defended the same thesis as I had in 1958. Concerning ethics he wrote: "The idea that ethics is a theological or philosophical study of norms for human behaviour stems from pagan thought and obstructs efforts toward radical reformation of non-ethical sciences."

While I would not express my opinions so strongly, I think this statement of Van der Stelt is essentially correct. Broadly speaking, no general or special science can formulate the concrete practical norms for any sphere of life. Science is not our guide to living. The children of God should be, and are in fact, guided by the Word and Spirit of God.

And if we are not guided by the Word and Spirit

26

of God, then no science will guide us. Our primary motivation will come from the spirit of the humanistic world which, in fact, already plays the guiding role in our modern, Western culture.

Why, then, do we study and teach ethics? Let me offer an explanation. All the special sciences, but most of all the so-called "humanities," are inevitably operating with concepts, schemes, methods, and patterns of thought that are basically moulded by philosophy. This is the very nature of philosophy. It provides us with very general insights and concepts.

Within philosophy there are no parts, isolated themes, or fields in the strict sense of the term. Philosophy is a science of totality. It is guided by what have been called transcendental ground-ideas in which the content of the philosopher's faith enters his investigations.

All the special sciences, and particularly the humanities, have their cosmological, anthropological and praxiological presuppositions. Therefore, all the sciences need their own special philosophical prolegomena, from which they always borrow fundamental insights into human life and human praxis.

In my opinion, then, there is still a legitimate place in theology for a special theological ethics. But what does this mean? What is the task of such ethics?

I believe the task of theological ethics is to investigate, in a specific theological way, what the Bible says about practical human life. In this context,

27

the role of theological ethics is to investigate the patterns of daily life in biblical times as they relate to the commandments, statutes and judgements of God given in the Scriptures.

I believe this is a very important task because the so-called "catalogues of vices and virtues" in the New Testament, for example, offer a profound guide to our hearts and to our basic attitude toward life. I do not consider theological ethics to be a special discipline alongside dogmatics and exegesis; it belongs to both dogmatics and exegesis and, beyond these, to church history as well. The doctrine of sanctification is also a fundamental issue in theological ethics.

With these thoughts in mind, I hope to pursue a philosophical survey of the Christian ethos.

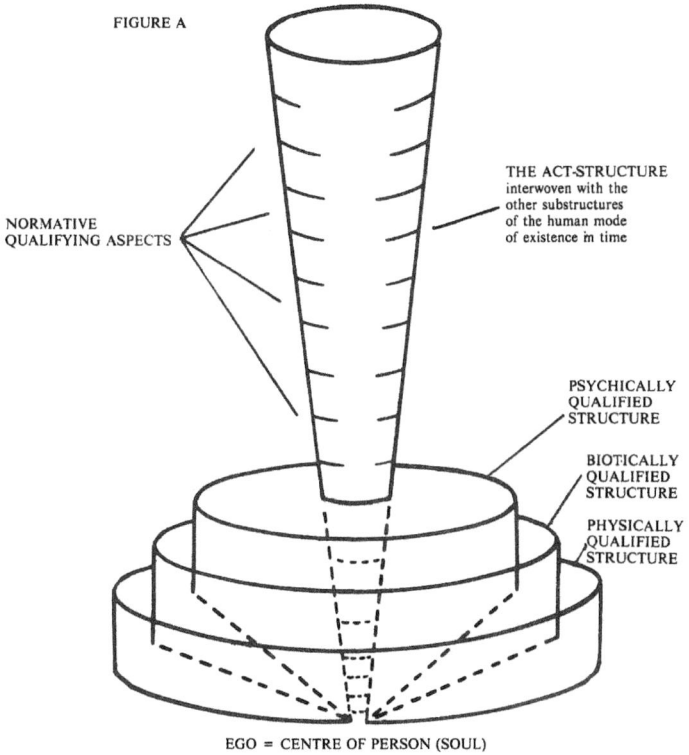

FIGURE A

NORMATIVE
QUALIFYING ASPECTS

THE ACT-STRUCTURE
interwoven with the
other substructures
of the human mode
of existence in time

PSYCHICALLY
QUALIFIED
STRUCTURE

BIOTICALLY
QUALIFIED
STRUCTURE

PHYSICALLY
QUALIFIED
STRUCTURE

EGO = CENTRE OF PERSON (SOUL)

FIGURE B
CROSS-SECTION OF THE STRUCTURE OF HUMAN ACTS

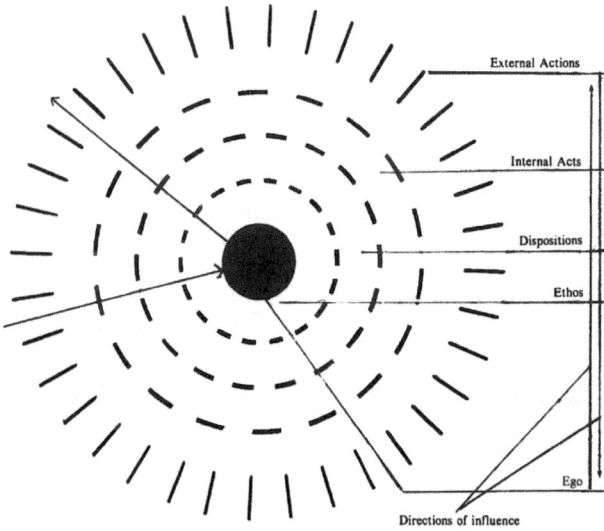

External Actions

Internal Acts

Dispositions

Ethos

Ego

Directions of influence

FIGURE C – DEPTH-SECTION OF THE STRUCTURE
OF HUMAN ACTS

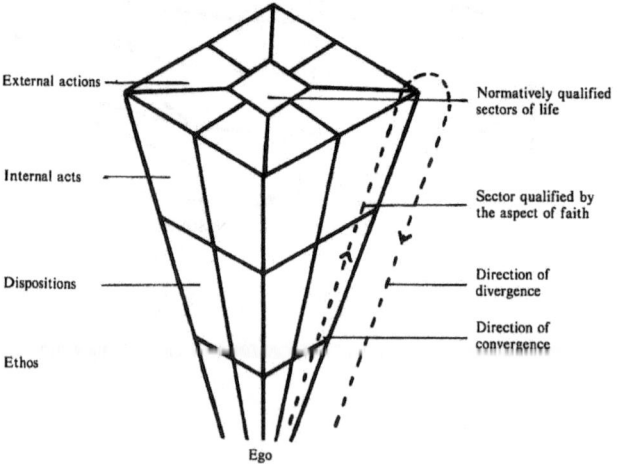

External actions

Internal acts

Dispositions

Ethos

Ego

Normatively qualified
sectors of life

Sector qualified by
the aspect of faith

Direction of
divergence

Direction of
convergence

30

FIGURE D
HUMAN LIFE (PRAXIS)

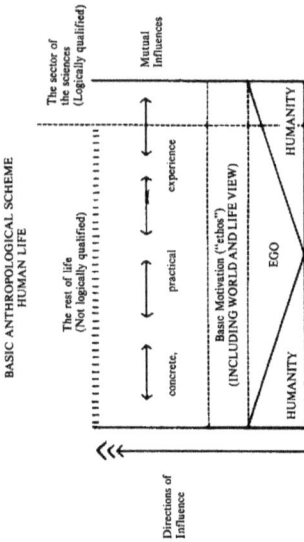

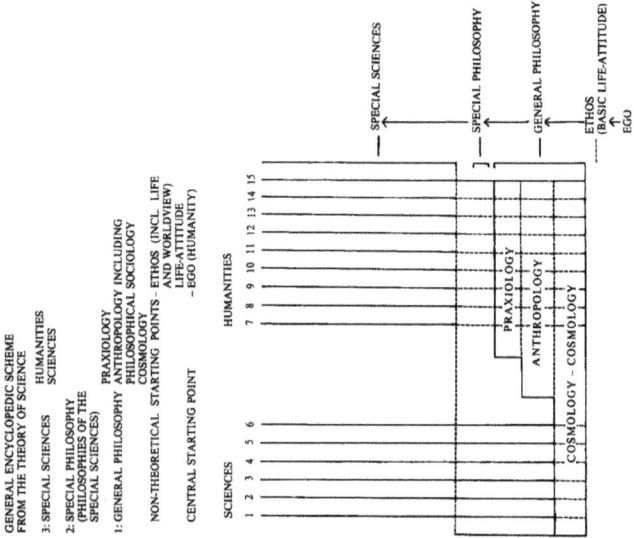

31

CHAPTER 2

The Relation Between the Revelation of Creation and Word-Revelation[1]

Formulation of the Problem

MY SUBJECT IS an old and well-known issue in theology; in science it is as problematic as ever. It is usually formulated in theology as the relation between general and special revelation. To raise this issue in these terms might seem to indicate that Reformational philosophy has something new and important to say on this matter. In any case, I do hold this view.

In 1951 a volume of the dogmatic studies of G.C. Berkouwer was published under the title *General Revelation*. At that time I mentioned in a short review of this splendid book that I regretted how Berkouwer maintains the distinction between general and special

---

1. Rewritten and amplified paper read on the International Philosophical Symposium 16-19 August 1976, at Driebergen, organised by the Vereniging voor Calvinistische Wijsbegeerte.

revelation.[2] I will now take the opportunity to explain and elaborate on my earlier comments.

In the light of a preliminary Christian epistemology, we shall first have to look at how the problem is stated. We can begin by noting the heading for this chapter. What is this problem? Is the problem stated correctly, and to what extent? At the end of this chapter a further question will be posed: what is the value of a treatise on this problem?

First, does this issue deal with a practical faith-question or a typical "problem" in theoretical thought? Stated differently, is it about an elucidation of faith and a witness to faith? Or are we concerned primarily with a scientific-theological reflection? The one question does not exclude the other. But because two activities are mentioned here (faith and science) and their natures must be properly distinguished, we must be aware of our present intention and of what we consider of *primary* importance.

I should begin with a disclaimer. The epistemological distinction between non-theoretical and theoretical thought cannot be treated here in detail. It is a premise borrowed from the philosophy of logics, namely the theory of cognition. But it is possible in practical faith to ask questions about the relation between God's Word and God's deeds and, more than this, to witness to this relation in preaching or confession, for example. However, my interest here is in a Christian-scientific reflection on

---

2.   *Sola Fide*, Vol. 5, no. 1 (Jan. 1952) p. 22.

the "problem" at hand.[3]

There is something strange about the distinction between faith and theology. In many Christian traditions no attention is given to such a distinction, and both terms are used interchangeably. But many theologians have voiced a difference between the two; priority has been given to faith, which in our opinion is seen correctly as the basic condition for good theology. Occasionally theology is relativized with regard to faith. In the case of different theological and ecclesiastical interpretations, people still "know" that they are "one in faith." There is a longstanding tradition that these differences are "just gradual."

Sometimes we speak very uncritically of "theologically accounted for" confessions and religious faith-ideas. In such expressions, the norm is said to lie more or less consciously in *theology as a science*. Faith is only healthy (i.e., biblically founded and free from heresy) if it is theologically (i.e., scientifically) well "accounted for." Even in these circles, where the sciences are treated with partly healthy mistrust, an exception is made for theological science. Theological science is acceptable, as long as it leaves intact a certain number of fundamental "doctrines of faith" (including the *theological* doctrine

3. Although in communication the distinction between a "question" and a "problem" should be treated with great flexibility, we find that when treating real questions there is an insistent tendency in our personal language to distinguish between practical and scientific or theoretical questions. Theoretical questions we preferably call "problems," a term we try to avoid when treating practical questions.

35

of "verbal inspiration").

We intend to treat the stated problem philosophically and theologically, on the basis of an *a priori* faith in the unity of God's actions, deeds and words, both "universal" and "particular." On this basis, we come to a critique of the given problem. We also confront theological efforts to find a unity in a so-called "harmonious connection" of "general" and "special" revelation. Naturally, in the face of all kinds of heresies we appreciate the good intentions of efforts to combine them. On the level of faith we associate ourselves closely with these efforts. But similar problems arise in the suggestions of a "bi-unity" if it concerns body and soul in anthropology, or in the case of horizontalism and verticalism, matter and spirit, nature and grace, etc.

In our scientific thought we can strive to heal our fancied dualities which apparently, inevitably and with inner necessity lead to dialectical (in the sense of conflicting) *dualisms*. In wavering and subtle syntheses these components always try to deny one another the primacy in a *theoretical dialectics*. They do so because in the religious depth-dimension of scientific thought (ethos, ground motive) at least two principles of origin are active, and these exclude one another.

The Religious and the Theoretical Dialectic of Nature and Supra-Nature

The thesis that I want to explain and defend here concerns the distinction between general and special revelation. I find the most common elements of this distinction to be untenable from my theological position. In contrast, I advocate a unity-view, which theologically trained readers perhaps will consider a "christomonistic" view. (In our time "christomonistic" thought is ascribed to Karl Barth and his school.)

At this stage I should like to call attention to this term. Such "christomonism" is just as far removed from my standpoint as, for example, its modern counterpart, seen in the views of H. M. Kuitert. With both of these opposite views I have external points of contact. We deviate from the classic reformed, theological tradition. According to Barth, "nature" disappears eschatologically in "grace." For Kuitert the belief that the Holy Scriptures are the "special Word-revelation" is almost denied as supranaturalism and metaphysics in favour of "general revelation" *cum annexis*. Here we are making an effort to eliminate the antithesis in this distinction from a Reformational philosophy. Our work must be seen as *one* of the tokens that this philosophy is on the way to conquering the forces of the age-old religious *and* theoretical dualism of nature and grace (as opposed to supranaturalism).

Under the influence of Dooyeweerd, the heading of this sub-section mentions "religious" dialectics.[4] This subject must be clearly distinguished from the theological variants of the scheme of nature and

---

4. Cf. *Reformatie en Scholastiek in de wijsbegeerte* I, 1949, A., par. 2. "The relation between religious and theoretical dialectics," pp. 41-46.

grace rooted in it. In many ways the theologies of our age (both Roman Catholic and Protestant) try to break through this scheme. They offer two extremes: either reducing nature to supra-nature (as opposed to grace) or the opposite. The course of development of theology through the ages shows the continuous shifting of the primacy between the two *poles* of natural and supra-natural, of nature and grace, held together in dialectical synthesis. The accent shifts in the permanent succession of so-called "one-sided" reactions, which invariably summon each other.

On the other hand, diverse "monistic" efforts were always criticized for "speculation." Berkouwer, for example, offers in *General Revelation* (Grand Rapids, Michigan, 1979 6th edition), the following comments:

> It goes without saying, that attempts have repeatedly been made to establish a unity and harmony between general and special revelation. Such attempts were always beset with various dangers. Thus it was possible to reduce the area of God's universal activity and to permit it to become obscured behind the particular acts of God. Then, too, the particular doings of God could become so obscured that they were no more than a transparent aspect of God's universal activity. Or again, it was possible by means of an exaggerated supra-lapsarianism to conceive of the unity of God's doings

in a Christological, Christocentric synthesis. The striking thing about all such views is the fact that they always terminate in *speculation*. Accordingly, one can arrive at a speculative view of the general revelation of God, or it is possible to conclude, from the viewpoint of eternity, that the Logos would have assumed human nature even without the fall. In contrast with all such views, however, the Scriptures teach us to be modest in our thinking, also in seeking a synthesis. They limit us to the utterances of God to prevent us from going astray in our thinking. Within these limitations we know by faith the unity of all God's doings (pp. 306, 307).

Berkouwer goes on to say:

In him the sovereign unity of God's universal and particular activity is contained. But confessing this unity by faith is quite different from perceiving and comprehending it. If the human mind insists on comprehending the dual character of God's actions, then it always ends in one of two ways: either it proceeds from the universal acts of God and declares the particular actions to be superfluous, or at best grants them illustrative value; or it proceeds from the particular deeds of

> God and represents the *majesty* of God
> as being exclusively present in the sign
> of the cross, and the power of God in
> cross and resurrection.

We are struck by Berkouwer's warning about the danger of speculation. This warning acquires a special meaning for us because speculation in general, and especially the "speculation of unity," is often ascribed to philosophy from a positivistic idea of science. In fact, classic Reformed theologians (D. Bonhoeffer among others) often heard the reproach of "Offenbarungs-positivismus," which was not always completely unfounded. Much of modern theology orientates itself openly to neo-positivistic thought patterns. (I am thinking here of Hubbeling, Brummer, Kuitert and others.)

The "Speculative Unity-Tendency" of Philosophy and the Theological Basis for the Distinction between General and Special Revelation

From classical times to the present, most philosophers have been aware that philosophical thought is directed to the unity of the existing world ("ens et unum convertuntur").[5] Nevertheless, one can always

---

5. To choose only one of the countless explanations:
   "Das hervorragende Interesse in der Einheit ergab sich aus der Natur des Philosophierens selbst . . ."
   K. Flash in: HIST. WTB. der Philosophie 2, 1972 column 367. We should prefer to reverse this and explain philosophy's inevitable alignment to unity from the dynamic unity

see the hesitancy or hear the dislike for "philosophy's speculative thought on unity" in periods of resignation and/or irrationalism.

This objection is often directed to the "Philosophy of the Cosmonomic Idea," even though Dooyeweerd analysed the perspectival structure of the different "horizons" of unity and totality more extensively than most other philosophers.[6] An important aspect of the resistance to this philosophy is directed toward its central point: the faith-insight in the philosophically formulated "transcendent radical (root) unity of the cosmos in Christ Jesus." In biblical terms, "All things are created and exist together in Christ" (Col. 1:16-17).

Only through this insight do we find a way to counter the religious dialectics which in different historical and theoretical forms and schemata govern our Western way of life and way of thinking. What matters most in this issue is a philosophical view of reality. For this reason, the Reformational revolution of the idea of creation sheds a new light on the meaning of "nature." This notion will be discussed in the following paragraphs, but first we should take stock of the general theological grounds for the incorrect or less correct distinction between general and special revelation.

Berkouwer discusses this distinction between

---

of the uni-versum itself.

6. Cf. his paragraph that begins "The levelling constructive scheme of the whole and its parts" (*A New Critique of Theoretical Thought* III, 424).

general and special revelation in detail and rejects many of the past alternatives. His book is very valuable and significant for the theological discussion on "general revelation," but unfortunately the view to which we adhere in this context is not discussed.[7]

Berkouwer quite correctly claims that sin and its consequences gave rise to our notion of a special revelation:

> This historical aspect in our discussion of God's revelation (the fall) also helps to explain why theologians have repeatedly discussed special revelation in relation to the fall and to the period after the fall (p. 308).

After having mentioned the fall, Berkouwer offers the following comments:

> God reveals himself *anew*, in an historical act of mercy, in the revelation of the enmity which he posits and which is consequently an act of reconciliation. In this revelation lies the beginning of the particular dealings of God, which, in the midst of the universal doings of God among all peoples, paves the way for the particularism of salvation in Israel and the proclamation of his salvation *exclusively* to Israel (p. 310).

---

7. Cf. J. C. van der Stelt: Philosophy and Scriptures, doctoral thesis, Dordt College 1978.

Further on he says the church speaks of the *new*, *special* revelation of God in light of the guilt and lost state of humanity. This train of thought does not in any way deny the connection between the so-called general and special revelation or disregard it.

In this regard Berkouwer reminds us of Kuyper, who speaks of the special revelation in strong terms. Kuyper uses words such as "accidental," "revelation-aid" and even the "abnormality" of special revelation. These expressions are only meant and understood in the context of guilt and alienation.

Both Kuyper and Berkouwer turn against "juxtaposition or co-ordination of general and special revelation" and against declaring both independent:

> The natural theology of Rome creates the impression that nature (created reality) *was intended* to function independently as a reality, from which man could conclude to its first cause, if need be without Word-revelation. However, that is not at all the case. Whatever is severed in the course of history (because of the fall of man) belongs together according to God's original purpose and revelation. And for this reason we speak of special revelation as a *new* revelation (p. 313).

Berkouwer's argument ("for this reason") may sound strange, but in my opinion it can be understood. We simply need to consider the strong accent Berkouwer puts on the "*historical aspect*" of our pronouncements on God's revelation *and* of God's revelation itself. What is "new" in the "*special*" revelation is connected with the situation changed by the fall. Yet we are still not able to speak of a correction of, or even an "extension" or "supplement" of, general revelation. What is "new" about *special* revelation is the revelation of God's compassion for a lost and alienated humanity. For the time being He is concerned with "particular" people – the elected – and therefore his dealings with them are "exclusive."

We presume it is clear, from the fragments of Berkouwer's argument quoted here, that he does not intend to declare general revelation as a separate, independent source of knowledge. It is not possible for reason, without faith, to come to a certain although perhaps incomplete "natural" knowledge of God.

It is strange that Berkouwer sees the historical *aspect* of revelation, and the "new"-ness of the special or particular revelation of God's compassion which functions in it, as a sufficient basis to maintain a duality in the revelation of God: universal and particular. He takes pains to reject various misconceptions which imply an independent "general" revelation. In the face of efforts to reach a "unity-version," he posits only justified warnings on the basis of the history of theology and its effect in practice. He offers no other alternative than "the *harmony* in the testimony of Scripture on general and special Revelation." He merely warns that we must not try to penetrate with our thought the unity in both God's revelations, which we explicitly confess.

According to Berkouwer, the duality of the revelation-actions must always be acknowledged in the present distinction. This is done not for the sake of subtle "speculation" in a theoretical passion for distinction, but as a *confession* of breach and guilt.

On this point Berkouwer seems to waver. First he says:

> He who attempts to go beyond faith in making a comprehensible rational syn-thesis, *fuses two* matters . . . *which can be differentiated by us only in the light of the Scrip-tures* (italics added).

In place of the dots stand these remarkable words: "*which historically are not discrete in the dealings of God.*" However, shortly thereafter we read:

> Word and deed revelation are sundered in the historical course of history . . . Whatever is severed in the course of his-tory (because of the fall of man) belongs together according to God's original pur-pose and revelation.

At one point we learn that these revelations *are not discrete*, but several pages later they are *severed*.

Hence we find that the eventual theological search for unity in the revealing acts of God is characterised by Berkouwer as an attempt "to go beyond faith in making a comprehensible rational synthesis."

We do not allow ourselves to become disheartened by this, although I am deeply convinced of the very often rationalistic transgression of bounds which is also prevalent in orthodox theology. Here a "rationalistic synthesis" that transcends faith is expressed more traditionally than Berkouwer intended. In so far as we wish to have our *thought directed* theologically and philosophically to the unity, and wish to be directed consciously by the *confessed* unity, we do not go any further than to speak with Mekkes of the "lower side" of faith:

> She (theology) cannot go further in the concept-formation than (given) distinctions of boundaries, in which the comprehending hand may not close itself around *that* which it takes hold of, but only touch the lower side in modesty whereby only a limited transparency and no single "synthetic" insight or oversight can be obtained.[8]

Again, we do not differ with Berkouwer on this *confessional*, concrete level of faith. But *theologically* we ask ourselves why Berkouwer did not study the often mentioned *faith* that the two revelations belong together as an "object" of deepened reflection. He confesses faith in their unity, although to him it cannot be fathomed and penetrated by "speculative"

8. J. P. A. Mekkes, *Scheppingsopenbaring en Wijsbegeerte,* 1961, p. 56.

thought from an "urge for synthesis." By following Berkouwer's example we would indeed split our confession. The unity of these revelations in God would be separated from theological thought, which is bound to the historical diversity.[9]

This issue touches on the philosophical view of reality inherent in every theology. It also concerns the encyclopedic, theological, cognition-problem of the philosophy of religion. By this I mean the diversity on the one hand, and the deeper unity in the diversity on the other, implied in the relation between faith and theology. We must suffice by quoting the rest of the already mentioned pronouncement of Mekkes. The concluding part of the citation is directly applicable to the theological problem at hand:

> The insight that moves theology and which alone can lead her contemplations in faithfulness to Scripture, is a comprehension through faith. But faith, however er spiritually clear in its distinctions, does not surrender its mystery to whatever theoretical consideration. When creation as such already erects its insurpassable barriers to the imperiousness of reason, then it does this in the first instance to the side where God directly and rightly demands surrender and nothing else.

9. That we do not agree on this point is therefore rather exceptional, because we usually have more trouble with the blending or even with the barely or not effective distinction of faith and theology in orthodoxy.

A Christian-Philosophical Basic Conviction Regarding the Way of Existence of the Cosmos

Reformational philosophy and "orthodox" Christian theology both confess in *faith* that the world was created by God. They also hold that this one Creator-God reveals *Himself* in all His works to human beings, whom He created in His image and likeness.

A difference of opinion exists, however, on the way in which this faith works through and becomes practicable in the scientific vision of reality, i.e., how one sees the relation between God and the cosmos. The God of the philosophers is not implied here. I am speaking of the living God in what He does and says on the one hand, and the concrete *existence* and *mode of existence* of creatures, including human life and society, on the other hand.

Surely a common confession of creation and of the implied sovereignty of God does exist. We can come to agreement about His power and authority over all creation and of the total dependence of creatures, individually and in their mutual relations, on God. That is the substance of the Christian faith and confession, based on the revelation of God in His Word – the Bible. This is faith-knowledge founded on the analytically differentiated moment (or "element") – the actual act of believing and confessing.

This knowledge element in faith can be theoretically abstracted from the concrete faith-act. It can be analysed scientifically and objectively, not in

48

reality but in abstraction from the full reality of faith. The result is a separate, theoretical concentration on the question of what can be said analytically, precisely, and clearly about the nature and mode of existence of the creature.

Our concern here is more than what is given expression in the Word-revelation to faith as implicit knowledge, and more than the Bible commissions us to believe. The theoretical attention is not directed only to "biblical data" for specific faith-knowledge, but directs itself "empirically" to the *rest* of creation.

Because of our *preceding* knowledge of Scriptures, the order and laws discovered by an investigating mind are immediately understood non-theoretically by faith as a revelation of God's creational will. Many texts describe God's commands, His way of creating things, as if they were in existence already. God speaks and it is there, He commands and it comes into being, He wills and it happens. The order and the law, like the historical course of events experienced as a blessing or a verdict, are noticed at all times. They are observed wherever the scope of human experience is religiously and philosophically contemplated.

In various religions and philosophies man busied himself with this study. From this experience and from the contemplation of existence, some variant of the idea of a world-order (mostly in connection with the divine power) has emerged.

In the Veda-period of the old Indian religion, this world-order was called *rta* and was associated

49

with the god Varuna. In the period after the Vedas, *rta* was replaced by the narrower concept *satya*, which is limited to the moral order and the order in knowledge and truth. In Buddhism the order in the world events is expressed by the word *dharma*. These Indo-Iranic concepts also correspond to the old Chinese thought of *tao*. This idea of order was elaborated more universally by Lao-tse and, as a kind of social conscience, by Confucius. This idea of order is comparable to what in old Egypt was called *ma-at*, an order in the cosmos guaranteed altogether by the sun-god *Re* and in the narrower circle of state-life by various *kings*. The Sumerians knew the eternal, ever-constant world-order which they denoted with *me*. The Russian concept *prawda* has the same connotation, but with a more social-ethical accent: truth and reliability.

In contrast, Christianity speaks of creational ordinances and ordinations, together with a view of the unity and coherence of *the creational order*. One of the main characteristics of Reformational philosophy is this biblically inspired idea of the creational order, with all its cohering but distinguishable laws and norms. This idea is elaborated frequently in comparisons and confrontations with detailed studies of the special sciences. It confronts what has been understood and assimilated historically by philosophers with reference to the *nature and structure* of reality.

One of the most fundamental points of

difference between the traditional views of reality can be summarised as the rejection by Christian philosophy of the idea of substance. This idea has a religious-dualistic origin in ancient heathen Greece. No metaphysical concept had so much influence in theology (Christology, ecclesiology, doctrine of sacraments, ethics) than the concept *substance*, the Latin translation of the Greek hypostasis, often equivalent to "being" (ousia). "Substance" means that which exists in-dependent, in itself and of itself, without any "sustaining ground."

We cannot even consider a broad outline of the philosophical problem inherent in this concept. We can only conclude that in spite of the replacement of the substance-concept by function-concepts in the natural sciences and the social sciences, non-Christian thought still bases its arguments on the substance-concept, viewed unconsciously in its original religious sense. In this view, reality is abstracted and severed from its sustaining creational order, which is the ever-valid Creator's will of the living God.

The most important characteristic of Reformational philosophy in reference to the view of reality is the inviolable and mutual "correlation" of the subject-side and the law-side of reality. On the law-side of reality lies its dynamics, its ground, its *directedness* to the Creator (being "created-for-God"). Here God reveals Himself in *all* existence, in *all* the "works of His hands." The text of Romans 1:20 proclaims that God's "eternal" power and His "divine nature" (dunamis and theiotés) can be known. Here God manifests His many-sided will and being in the abundance of the creational ordinations. These cause all things to be *what* they are and *as* they subjectively are, namely determined by and directed to the law-side, God's "dynamis."

Out of the spiritual compulsion of the heathen substance-concept came the *dualistic* view of the relation between God and creature. This view expresses itself in a dilemma: either God *or* the creature. Indeed, God and creature are two. Contrary to every form of pantheism, this viewpoint can be maintained philosophically and theologically. This duality becomes clear as soon as we realise that the creature can be pictured as standing on his own or independently (i.e., as a substance). The creature is separated from and eventually opposed to God's will, which is the permanent active sustaining ground, the propelling power, the valid life-law for all creatures. According to Reformational insight, the expression "created substance" is a contradiction.

Here we can still add another point. In the beginning the initiators of the Philosophy of the Cosmonomic Idea often designated the law of God as the "boundary between God and cosmos."[10] This

10. Cf. article 2 of the Statutes of the Vereniging voor Calvin-
    isme en de Reformatie van de Wijsbegeerte 1933, pp. 23-
    25. Dooyeweerd seldom uses the expression. The register
    of his principal work mentions one instance only. In my
    opinion a backsliding into a metaphysical law-ontology can
    take place in terms of the above-mentioned expression,
    which provides a point of contact with the Scholastic tra-

formulation can be misinterpreted in several ways, but it denotes what has been written in connection with the relation between God and creature. Every theoretical hypostatization (declaring the creature independent of God) *tears the creature to pieces* (theoretically because it considers the subjective side separate from and opposite to the law which is then declared independent and self-supporting). This cannot be rectified by calling the law an inner natural or metaphysical law; the crevice cannot be concealed any longer.

Christians ought to argue against this line of thinking. They should also guard against making the law-side an independent, self-supporting, metaphysical domain of norms and values, a world-order of natural right or a "logos" (as opposed to logical world-order). In God we live and move (Acts 17:28) in the diversity and fulness of the revelation of His will as creator, judge and redeemer. There is no nature *an sich*, no creature on its own.

Genuine science is mistaken when it views reality as limited to its subjective-side or to its law-side. In both cases we can see a serious reduction, a theoretical declaration of independence or a substantialization. This is also true when the metaphysical substance-concept is replaced by function-concepts. Regardless of the concrete functions of objects, social communities, institutes or happenings, their subject-side has an indestructible correlation with their

dition in theology. (Cf. *A New Critique of Theoretical Thought* I, p. 99).

normative law-side.

There is a theoretical problem of constancy and variability in *all* reality. But there is also the dilemma of a rigid interpretation of natural laws and of the "moral" natural law on the one hand and, as a necessary reaction, a functionalistic relativism (also part of the divine creator's will) which underrates, misinterprets, or denies all constancy on the other hand.

A contemplation of reality detached from God ("etsi Deus non daretur") inevitably leads to such a dilemma. H. Schultze[11] made a commendable effort to distinguish divine institutions or mandates and the human positivizing of these in various social institutes. He also effectively criticized the traditions of natural rights and the theology of the creational ordinances.

Yet, for the greater part, his work ended in the failure of a personal solution. His sharp dualism of general and special revelation, of the two domains or regiments of God, of God's left hand and God's right hand, dominate his view of reality and man, to which he ascribes a structural "Doppeldimensionalität." The whole vision of Schultze illustrates the intrinsic interlacing of anthropology and cosmology. Combined, they act as the "floor" under the special sciences, including sociology and theology with its

---

11. Hans Schulze, *Gottesoffenbarung und Gesellschaftsordnung. Untersuchungen zur Prinzipienlehre der Gesellschaftstheologie*, Miinchen, 1968. Cf. my contribution in 1969 in Philosophia Reformata.

differentiated areas.

The General Character of the Revelation of God: The Revelation of Creation

On the basis of God's Word, those who hold to Christian faith believe that the will of God revealed in the creational order is of universal validity. His will is the sustaining "ground" of all existence. Only man is created in such a way that he is *naturally and consciously directed* to God's will. In the dynamics of his life through God Himself, man received this normative structural direction, being created "for God."

For this reason, there is a religious and scientific directedness toward the "deeper ground," which is a stimulus to our existence and constitutes its driving force (the dunamis and theiotés of Rom. 1:20). God reveals Himself in and through His creating acts (including the preservation and supreme rule) in such a way that "they would look for him, and perhaps find him as they felt around for him. *Yet* God is actually not far from any of us . . ." (Acts 17:27).

In this quotation there is a reference to a strange discrepancy between the creationally-essential "look for Him," who is so powerfully near, and the qualifying line "Yet we live *in* Him." How is it possible that He must be looked for in such an endless way by all nations, in all centuries, and in futility as people "feel around," *getting no hold?*

The answer lies in the great self-concealment of God, in His *wrath* and thus in the *darkness in our human hearts* (Rom. 1:18, 21). Instead of re-discovering God – and thereby himself, as befits man according to his nature – man gropes about and does not get hold of anything. He seeks and does not find; his autonomy becomes a tragic and ridiculous "losing himself," even in that which man sees as his own grandeur, his *thought*, his "deliberations" (Rom. 1:21). His nature has become unnatural "and their *empty minds* are filled with darkness" (Rom. 1:21).

Many orthodox theologians have correctly noted how the text of Romans 1 points to the guilt of man; he does not understand and believe the so-called general revelation. This fact does not minimise the revelation of God. Berkouwer even refers with approval to C. van Til, who dares to speak of the *sufficiency* of general revelation even if we, *by our own fault*, do not find it sufficient. We fail to reach the true knowledge of God through general revelation not due to revelation, but due to ourselves!

It has become common practice in theology to call the general revelation "universal," as distinct from the "particular" of the special revelation. We shall presently discuss the criterion for this distinction. For now we need only state that there is no difference of opinion about "universal" or creation-revelation as far as the contents, address and means or channels of this revelation are concerned. God directs Himself by way of the "works of His hands" in "nature and history," thereby including the *words* that God spoke to Adam, to *all* people and even perhaps to angels and devils. God reveals Himself in His "eternal power and divine nature." That is the universality of the revelation of God in, through and to the creatures, the *generality and universality of the creation law*, the life-order, the being as they should be of creatures from, by and to God. This is the meaning of being.[12]

The general and universal revelation of God reveals His "virtues" in the way these become manifest in the creator's will. God's virtues are also seen in the diversity, coherence, and unity of the total creation-order, in which the will of God the creator is expressed clearly. (We include here the historical formation of power and language.)

That general revelation is also known after the fall is clear from the Bible: "Gentiles do not have the law (in the same historical form as Israel), but whenever of their own free will they do what the law commands, they are a law to themselves, even though they do not have the Law" (Rom. 2:14).

Western theologians have always had difficulty explaining how the world was created by God *in Christ*. H. N. Ridderbos remarks on this problem: "On the *en auto entidthe* exists uncertainty and

---

12. Expressed in the familiar words of Dooyeweerd on the first pages of his principal work: "This universal character of *referring* and *expressing*, which is proper to our entire created cosmos, stamps created reality as *meaning*, in accordance with its dependent non-selfsufficient nature. *Meaning* is the *being* of all that has been *created* and the nature even of our self-hood. It has a religious root and a divine origin." *A New Critique of Theoretical Thought* I, p. 4.

57

difference of opinion."[13] The creation in Christ does not seem to be that difficult to understand, because we are aware of how the Scriptures describe the reign of Christ. Everything the Scriptures say about the creation in Christ is accommodated by Karl Barth in a soteriological way. This posits a "christomonism," christocentrism and christocracy *within* the dialectic of grace and nature; inevitably a reaction was bound to follow.

We witness this reaction *even* by previously fervent followers of Barth, often through a phase of transition, similar to Bonhoeffer's or sometimes via the teachings of Tillich. For a long time Reformed theologians tried to play the so-called "cosmic" and "soteriologic" meaning of Christ against each other. We think of Berkouwer's book on general revelation, of Grosheide in his commentary on the Gospel of John and of Ridderbos in his commentary on Colossians.

These attempts do not seem to have succeeded in spite of their authors' best intentions. These theologians have tried to unify both "aspects" in such a way that the "cosmological meaning," which is acknowledged in a barren, sterile orthodoxy in doctrine, is not recognised and defended and is completely forgotten. Theological ethics could not deal with this issue satisfactorily.

In 1965 Kuitert wrote that the views about the cosmic Christ generally concern "an effort to reach

13. Noted in his commentary on Colossians, p. 139.

that which the old theology had in mind, when they coined (or rather took over) the term, 'theologia naturalis' but then on a different basis".[14] A.G. Honig Jr. takes great pains (yet apparently without success) in his "De kosmische betekenis van Christus" (*The Cosmic Meaning of Christ*, Kamper Cahier 7, 1968) to come to a Christocentric view via the idea of the dominion of Christ. On the ecclesiastical reaction against all social, racial, and economic discrimination and on world-wide cooperation, he says: "In all these things realisations of God's intentions for this world can be seen as signs of the coming Kingdom. But no more than signs . . ."

The signs must, however, always be interpreted for us, because we cannot break away from the necessity to choose sides and make decisions. Indeed, we know in faith of the "concealed presence of God in history." "Ethics," the greatest theological crux of all times, again manifests itself clearly: "There is no clear and absolute authority for the interpretation of history. The church can be mistaken. We hope that the World Council of Churches will speak the right words for the sake of and in the name of the churches."

In other words, as long as the dialectic primacy lies with special revelation, the meaning of the "cosmic Christ" in this train of thought cannot be more than the biblical notions concerning the universal norms of justice, neighbourly love, freedom, peace, etc.

14. Cronicle in Geref. Theol. Tijdschrift, Vol. 65, 1965, p. 249 sq.

These are illustrated by the Mosaic legislation and especially through a "Jesulogy" from the life and works of Jesus, the New Man.

These notions find concrete substance when we concentrate on the typical economical, political, juridical, and moral questions and problems not only from the Word-revelation but also from the totality of the creational revelation, of which Christ is the "Beginning and the End." A scientifically re-formed Christian practice of special sciences, rather than theological ethics, is likely to offer us help. But even this approach is not the decisive answer.[15]

However, if the primacy in the dialectics of nature and grace shifts to "general" revelation, then natural (read un-natural) theology revives. Then the "church" again follows behind "the world," first in a practical way in "ethics" and then in a theoretical way. The syntheses between these two partialities can easily be detected in the essentially "Christian," docetic, and Baptist-utopian interpretations of what the Scriptures call the Kingdom of God. (In our times this is called freedom, equality, fraternity, community, justice, liberation, peace, and shalom by real, semi-

15. Van der Stelt (see above-note 7) advanced the following thesis:
"The idea that ethics is a theological or philosophical study of norms for human behaviour stems from pagan thought and obstructs a radical reformation of non-ethical sciences." This is a typical promotion-thesis which *must* be controversial. In fact, this thesis can be disputed because of a too radical formulation and because it lacks nuance. In principle, however, the thesis is correct.

and neo-Marxists. Through a personally tainted piety this "spirit" will easily pervade the churches.)

We should like to declare our confessional fellowship and solidarity with every theologian who tries to hold together as harmoniously as possible the two "aspects" – the cosmological and the soteriological, the universal and the particular. But *theologically*, these efforts are doomed. They have an anthropological cosmological "floor" underneath them. Indeed, they form a philosophical breeding-ground in which *two principles of origin* (substantial form and substantial material, freedom and nature) are split religiously in a dynamic dialectic of inspirations. These, in principle, cannot be brought into harmony; they continue to have an antagonistic correlation.

Theologically this dialectical-philosophical basis obtained its form in three ways: in an image of the relations between creation and redemption; through the doctrine of the two regiments of God's left and right hands; and also in the way some modern thinkers try to cover up the animosity between these two sources of knowledge of God, existing *next* to each other. By using Calvin's metaphor (the book of creation must be read through the spectacles of the Word-revelation), we can say that in the course of time the spectacles became more important than the book itself.

The disastrous theological consequences of juxtaposing the supposedly twofold revelational acts of God can only be prevented by looking at an alternative: the recognition of only *one* revelation-in-Christ, the Word, which was with God from the beginning. This self-revelation of God in His eternal Word retains its central position of source, fulness and transcendence in time if it manifests itself after the fall in the redeeming and liberating salvation-work of Jesus the Christ. God's self-revelation is always manifested *from* the divine Origin, who stays faithful to Himself and His creation in and beyond all times, through history till the "consummation" of "eternity."[16]

As Ridderbos quite rightly states in his previously mentioned commentary:

> Outside Christ every creature and every power is disintegrated. Only because and in so far as they are sustained by Christ and stand under His regime, do they have their cohering and meaningful relation with all other creatures. *Here the apostle indicates Christ as the sustaining ground and concentration point of all creatures and every power.*

---

16. Cf. also thesis 13 of Van der Stelt:

"To remove the tension in the relationship between creation and recreation, it is necessary to acknowledge the biblical revelation about the Logos as the Creation Word." This thesis forms the core of my article. But as a theological thesis it will presumably be disputed by many theologians. Therefore this "core" remains sterile if it only functions as a theological thought, when as a dynamic insight of faith it is not the inspiring centre of the whole reformational philosophical view of reality.

For Ridderbos the "cosmic meaning" of Christ is specially indicated in the "power and dominion" of Christ over all things and powers. But he does not explicitly relate this meaning to the dominion of Christ through the upholding, validating and completion of the will of God as it is revealed in the creation-order. This is the only way of clarifying the meaning of "being sustained." Only in this way will that part of the italicised passage from his commentary become actual in the created world.

In theology, the dominion of Christ ("To me is given all power on earth . . .") is forever severed from the creation-order by the inspiratory power of the nature-grace dualism. His dominion is separated from the creation-order in which the creator's and redeemer's dominion, as revelation of His will, come to us in work and word.

We shall conclude this sub-section with a few representative citations which illustrate how this dualism blocks the view of an inner unity, especially for those theologians who wish to cling to both "aspects" simultaneously. 1. "Der Wille Gottes als Grund der Gottesherrschaft ist nicht sozial institutionalisierbar. Damit entfällt fur eine evangelische Auffassung ein für allemal eine gesellschaftliche Theocratized."[17] 2. "Die Legierung der evangelische Botschaft mit irgendwelchen Strukturanalysen der Wirklichkeit bzw. mit philosophischen Konstruktionen kann einer evangelischer Theologie nur zum Schaden gereichen,

17. Hans Schulze, *Gottesoffenbarung und Gesellschaftsordnung*, p. 265.

ob es sich um dogmatische oder ethische Arbeiten handelt."[18]

The Contents of the Revelation of Creation

Since science emerged as an historical development of the intuitive knowledge, acquaintance and understanding of life, its task has been to refine, deepen and explicate the primary and implicit knowledge of the demands of the creational order. In scientific thought man dissociates himself, in the theoretical attitude of thought and knowledge, from primary experiential knowledge. He abstracts his object from the concrete context, limiting himself in his intentional interference to what can be distinguished analytically, i.e., what can be identified and possibly named.

In a similar way theology also busied itself with the exegesis and closer explanation of what God reveals of Himself both in the general and special revelation. In this regard the well-known discussion in Romans 1 and the expression "His eternal power and divine nature" are always central. In theology, as in many ecclesiastical confessions, it is customary in any commentary on the phrase "eternal power and divine nature" not to be restricted to these Greek *words*. The whole theological doctrine of the "virtues" or qualities of God is often associated with this text.

We rightly see in this short expression from Romans 1·20 an indication of much more. We could mention, for example, the Confessio Belgica (Dutch Creed). In article 1 a series of so-called qualities of God

18. O. Dillschneider, *Die evangelisch Tat*, 1940, pp. 16-17.

is mentioned, including eternal, incomprehensible, invisible, immutable, infinite, omnipotent, all-wise, righteous, and good. But an attentive reader will miss much of what he knows from the Bible. Therefore article 1 concludes this series with the general and encompassing phrase "and a very abundant fountain of all good (qualities)."

Article 2 quotes the expression "eternal power and divine nature" as an explication of the invisible things of God which we nevertheless contemplate in the big book of God's creation – sustenance and rule of all things, in which "all creatures, big and small, are like letters." The Catechism of Heidelberg in answer 122 uses the prayer: "Thee in all Thy works, in which Thy omnipotence wisdom, excellence, righteousness, mercy and truth are brought to light . . ." Obviously these confessions are not intended to be complete, or even "systematic," as is often the case in dogmatic surveys and classifications of the qualities of God. All this is irrelevant in this context.

In Protestant theology we seldom find a thorough consideration of the contents of general revelation. Rarely do we encounter its rich variety or the inner coherence between the divine life-laws for objects and the many distinctive actions and forms of society and humanity throughout history.

This comment is not meant as a reproach to theology; the broad elaboration noted above is not a legitimate task of theology, but of all other sciences. Theology, in our view, has to restrict itself to an elaboration of only *one* of the aspects of reality, namely the aspect of faith. All other aspects, including human and non-human phenomena of life-sectors qualified by it, are the field of non-theological special sciences.

What we can rightly expect from theology is that on *this point* it should not leave its task in default. Theologians must indicate the nature of creational ordinances as the *colourful and abundant will of God the creator*. A conscious refusal of theology to complete this task encourages both philosophy and the special sciences in their traditional *illusion*. They believe they can be "anti-metaphysical," autonomous on their own territory of scientific reason.

We should point out that theologians busied themselves with this problem in two ways. First, they were involved in the diverse designs of a "theology of ordinances of creation," in the subsequent combating of these theories and in some Protestant efforts to design a "Christian natural right." Second, theologians reflected critically on the thesis that the "natural sciences" (eventually supplemented by the "cultural sciences" or, in short, history) provide knowledge of *God* by means of the knowledge of nature, i.e., nature and history. (On the "theology of creational ordinations" I would refer readers to my article in *Philosophia Reformata* on "The Revelation of God and the Social Order," referred to in note 11 above.)

This second point requires our attention. It

concerns the rejection of a concept defended earlier: that natural science furnishes knowledge of God from the "general" revelation of God in "nature." (We omit the problem of "history" as a "source" of knowledge of God.)

From the abundance of literature, we again make use of the comprehensive text of Berkouwer to tackle these problems. Referring to this concept, Berkouwer says that man saw the Holy Scriptures as the book of the *special* revelation of God, and nature as the book of *general* revelation. Both theology and natural science are involved with the revelation of God. Berkouwer supports his argument with various quotations and footnotes. These make it clear that in the Calvinistic circle in our country up to approximately 1970, this was the predominant way of thinking. (I am referring to the work of W. J. A. Schouten, J. Lever, J. Verseveldt, Hooykaas, and authors from other countries and periods.)

Berkouwer, followed by many other theologians, argues against these ideas and rejects them completely. It is not sufficient to place the knowledge of nature on the same level as the knowledge of God's general revelation, because the revelation is about God *Himself*. Therefore, it is incorrect to say that natural science examines God's general revelation and also incorrect to say that *we owe the knowledge of God's revelation in nature to natural science.*

Berkouwer considers this notion to be a superficial attitude toward the concept and the reality of revelation. Indeed, general revelation concerns God's self-revelation and this, in Berkouwer's opinion, can only be known through faith and is not directed solely through scientific investigation.

Is a contradistinction posed here? If so, it is not necessary. Has Berkouwer not overlooked the *depth*-dimension of *all* knowledge, even of natural and scientific knowledge? Is a *division* between faith-knowledge and scientific knowledge not made too easily here? True, Berkouwer does not intend this division and he pleads for a recognition of the "original" unity of revelation. Indeed, Berkouwer thinks that the duality in God's revelation (general and special), caused historically by sin, does not suggest any independence, nor a competing or even a complementary relation between the two.

But *can* justice be done to the unity of origin of the revelation of God? Before we enter into this question critically, we acknowledge that Berkouwer sees the unity endangered precisely because of the two *kinds* of knowledge: natural scientific knowledge and faith-knowledge, which concentrate respectively on general and special revelation. He properly responds by saying the main subject at hand is knowledge of God, which is always and everywhere faith-knowledge. (Here readers may wish to consider the "Nature" psalms.)

We are left with a critical question. Did God reveal Himself in the works of creation? The natural scientists, among others, do not investigate creation from the *leading* viewpoint of faith. They work from the perspective of theoretically deepened *thought*, trying to unravel the secrets of creation. The intention of science is the revelation of *truth*. But doesn't theoretical *truth*, according to its structure, participate in the *full* Truth? And is not Christ the full Truth, as the Word of God?

Here one question is of primary importance. What does the "general" self-revelation of God reveal? Berkouwer also discusses this issue, so we will refer to his work presently. But first we want to emphasise three points: the so-called "general" revelation of God (a) is Word-revelation in Christ, the Logos, (b) has its origin in the triune God, and (c) when expressed philosophically *does not lose* its transcendent unity in Christ, but meticulously reveals it in history.

In theology, the unity in Christ of all creation, of the "universum" which is not chaos and not pluriversum, was pointed out by the "christomonism." The term "unity" is seen in the dualistic framework of the natural and the supernatural. It is used to explain the harmony and inner interdependence of both "revelations." This term is applicable to the well-known series of biblical texts in which the Word (Christ) is mentioned. In and through the Word, "all things" are created, have their permanence, their beginning and also their end, in the sense of fulfilment. (Textual examples can be found in John 1; Col. 1; Heb. 1:3, 11:3; 2 Cor. 4:6; Prov. 8; Rev. 3:14;

and Ps. 33:6). "The revelation of reality is indeed also a word-revelation."[19]

However, the arguments of theologians are not self-sufficient, *not even in their own sphere*. Indeed, what one quotes as "references" to prove that there are two revelations which are interdependent – naturally disposed to one another and which supplement each other – are only convincing to those who assume two revelations which differ in contents, means, character and address.

Berkouwer argues strongly that, as a result of human guilt and divine mercy, a *new special* revelation in history is added to the preceding, general, non-special revelation of creation. But he is not convincing. I hold to a view in which history has a supra-historical (also called "supra-temporal") centre in the transcendent "new" *Root* of David. This argument counters Berkouwer's theory. Christ was not only the Son of David *historically*, but also the pre-existing "Root of David and of the whole of the cosmos" (Rev. 5:5, 22:16) and thus of "the lineage" and progeny of David.

Here the meaning of the philosophical "floor" under theology is manifested. We do not want to <u>limit this</u> underpinning (as does Kuitert, for

19. So, for example H. Fries in: Mysterium Salutis. Dogmatiek in heilshistorisch perspectief I, (1967). p. 269.
   Cf. also my "Geen aardse macht", 1976, pp. 27-28, and among others: Hans Schulzez "Hinter dem menschlichen Handeln steht indessen die Dynamik der Ordinationes. Diese göttliches Schöpfungswort, das die soziale Hand-lung des Menschen begründet und trägt," ibid. p. 35.

example) to a "small anthropological floor." We do admit that Philosophical anthropology has a central place in philosophy. For this reason, it is important that we usually formulate the first two main themes of philosophy as a theory of structure, i.e., after the "prolegomena" we discuss anthropological cosmology and cosmological anthropology.

In my opinion this philosophical basis of theology, with its implicit view of history, is dualistic. On the one hand it distinguishes the historical aspect from all other ways of being and of experience, and on the other hand this basis does absolutize the historical aspect. All human life and even God's revelation is considered as "purely historical." The current and very general absolutizing of the historical aspect annuls itself logically, because no sensible answer can be given any more to the central question: "history of what?" The answer could not be history itself.

Here we should look at the history of the revelation of God. God's self-revelation entered time. Time, as something created, has a centre which is present always and everywhere, from the beginning till the end. This centre is the fulness of time, and the expression "supra-temporal" centre is only an expedient term. It has nothing to do with timelessness nor emptiness, nor with logical necessity. This centre is not more or less than the "Root" of the creation, Jesus Christ. He is the same yesterday, today and for all eternity, and therefore He is the fulness, origin, consummation, and fulfilment. The Scriptures say:

71

the alpha and the omega, the beginning and the end.

Theologians have always had trouble trying to explain the relation between Christ as time-transcending root of the cosmos and His historical work on earth. This problem emerges in almost all discussions on dogmatics: what is the relation between the justification from eternity, our sanctification in Christ, and "mortifying sin more and more"? What is the relation of the eternal predestination of God to human responsibility? How is Christ present in the earthly tokens of bread, wine and baptismal water? What is the relation between the one church of God, the "Body of Christ" and our many churches, or the one sin of Adam and our sins "in Adam"? What is original sin?

Berkouwer struggles frequently with these problems in the long series of his *Dogmatic Studies*. In my opinion he is partly handicapped by the deadly weight of the traditional immanence philosophy, which in the West sees reality as a matter of course. In this philosophy there is no real vision of the transcending centre of all earthly reality. Vollenhoven summarises all non-Christian philosophy in the term "functionalistic." He distinguishes heart and "function-mantle." Dooyeweerd speaks of "immanence philosophy" because he calls the central religious root of reality "transcendent," supra-temporal, being of *all* times and always transcending time.

If we take this view, it is possible to transcend

the present distinction between general and special revelation, with the theological connotations attached to all its variants. It is possible to know exactly the historical character of God's revelation in time and its progress in the direction toward the end. It is also possible not to limit God's revelation to the canon of Holy Scriptures, which is the radiating and directing centre of revelation.[20] This view leaves room for the acknowledgement of the redeeming and liberating acts of God in the history of peoples.

But such acknowledgement is not offered in the same way as in the current modernistic theology, which downgrades the universality of the salvation-Word of Christ in almost a semi-Marxist fashion. Salvation is said to be something that happens automatically in politics. Everything the Scriptures teach about the judgement by God of the heathen and of the faithless people (Israel and Christianity), even in connection with the last day, is ignored.

We can now understand the slight confusion which we noted in Berkouwer's book. He spoke first of God's revelation not being discrete and later of being sundered because through sin the novelty of

---

20. The following might be a good description of "biblicism": the lifting out and absolutising of the Bible from the whole of God's revelation of creation, which is given to us and addresses us in Christ as the integral Origin and End. In theological biblicism, a way of thought and a method of forming concepts are added which in exegesis, dogmatics and ethics are borrowed from "the" science, i.e., the methods of natural science. The so called "historical" method may be different, but not much better.

God's mercy was revealed – even in a "particular" way, exclusively to Israel. Depending on our point of view, we may also say that both positions hold true. God's revelation is the source, origin and eternal fulness of Him who reveals Himself in creation, in redemption and consummation, and His revelation is focussed on what manifests itself *historically* in the history of sin, faith and revelation. God's revelation concerns a "unity" which is one-in-Origin. As such, it concerns the ever-transcendent "unity-root" in which all historical *diversity* is concentrated and integrated.

Theologians could have profited enormously if they took the intrinsic time-character of reality and its supra-temporal transcending centre more seriously. Then they would no longer describe the central facts of the fall, the cross and the resurrection as purely historical facts. The salvation of God is indeed historical, but it is never tantamount to "pure history," the past. So here we are at the very root of the matter: it is (unintentionally) almost blasphemous to say that creation was an historical deed of God, because creation makes all historical facts possible. God's acts are "from eternity." Our time-bound concepts and ideas cannot be used to formulate nor to understand what this biblical term denotes.

The Revelation of Creation Includes Word-Revelation

The difference between God's deeds and words still serves frequently as a criterion for distinguishing general revelation from special revelation. Consequently, the terms *work-revelation* and *Word-revelation* were employed. But in my opinion, this criterion is arbitrary. It follows our practical experience when we sometimes note a contradiction between someone's words and deeds. Viewed philosophically, "words" as *language-deeds* have a different structure compared to non-lingually qualified activities. From the viewpoints of philosophy and the special sciences, the disparity in nature of differently qualified activities cannot be overlooked. Similarly, to absolutize this difference by ignoring the common *basis of unity* in the acting subject and in the law of God is equally unjustified.

Moreover, the more recent linguistic investigations of the Bible strongly suggest that word and deed in the Hebrew idiom can hardly be considered separately.[21] God's words are working words, creating words, words with effects in history. God calls into existence; He sends His breath and it becomes spring. Conversely, His deeds are well-spoken deeds, to such an extent that they are sometimes understood by heathen. Even outside Israel, people were mindful of the threats or the deeds of the mighty God of Israel.

From Genesis 1 we also know that God spoke to Adam. Hence there is no reason to characterise the so-called twofold revelation of God as work and Word revelation. A fundamental aspect of faith is the inner unity of God's creating speech, of what God still speaks in maintaining His creation and what He told Adam. This is the trustworthy truth of God

---

21. Cf. G. von Rad, Theol. des A. T., II, 1960, p. 93 sq.

which addresses man in the totality of his humanity.[22]

Scientific-philosophical investigation often pointed out the *referring* character of the diverse aspects of human and nonhuman existence. One could also find some support in the commentary of Ridderbos on the *sunesteken* – the co-existence of Christ – found in Col. 1:17. The theological-empirical investigation pointed out in many ways the "phenomenon" of human faith or "primordial faith" (Kuitert), without which no human existence seems possible. Kuitert calls this "small anthropological floor" the basis of theological detail. From an anthropological point of view, God Himself did create in man a "formal point of contact" (E. Brunner) to receive and understand the whole of the revelation of God's "dynamis and theiotes" (eternal power and divinity). Romans 1 says that the divinity is comprehended by man's reason from God's works. But in biblical usage there is certainly no anthropological distance between "reason" and "faith" as these must necessarily be distinguished in the sciences.[23] As far as a distinction

22. H. N. Ridderbos in his commentary on the letter to the Romans points out that from knowing God by the "nous" one must not "conclude that there would be in man in some or other way a 'province', that of reason, in which 'natural knowledge of God' would be present undefiled. More likely God's revelation to man *keeps pervading man in the indivisibility of his existence*" (Italics added) See also next note.

23. H. N. Ridderbos in his commentary "Aan de Romeinen," 1959, pp. 42-43.
"For the concept reason used here in Greek (nous) we have in fact no adequate expression. Nous in the religious

must be drawn, there is at the same time the "existing together" of Col. 1:17, the *coherence in Christ*.

In the religio-philosophical analysis of faith as a human way of experience, faith is not merely distinguished by Dooyeweerd (among others) from the logical analytical way of experience. He also compares faith to a window, just as Ridderbos does. "According to the order of creation this terminal aspect was destined to function as the opened window of time through which the light of God's eternity should shine into the whole temporal coherence of the world."

Dooyeweerd continues in the same vein:

> That this window has been closed by sin, and cannot be opened by man through his own activity, does not mean that it cannot be distinguished by the Divine power of the Holy Ghost (*A New Critique of Theoretical Thought* II, 1955, p. 302).

To describe God's Word-revelation as a second revelation, different from his *work*-revelation, is arbitrary and unjustified. So we cannot state that reason is the receiving-set of work-revelation, and faith is only meant for Word-revelation. Similarly, it

---

usage by Paul does not only indicate the knowing faculty, but man himself in his deepest inner selfconsciousness . . . In the nous lies the possibility for man to know God. It is, so to speak, the window, through which the light of God's revelation enters and by which man is addressed as responsible being."

is fundamentally incorrect to suggest a difference between the two "kinds" of revelation on the basis of the *contents*, the *what* of God's revelation. Perhaps Berkouwer had this in mind when he refused to speak of a "supplementary" revelation, namely of special revelation supplementing general revelation. The special revelation is not "an extension" of general revelation. (We might have had less trouble with these indications – supplement and extension – but much depends on one's point of view.)

If we posit one God who reveals Himself, we can speak of the inner unity of *all* God's revealing deeds, the "co-existence" in Christ. God expresses Himself in words and deeds in His Son; all things (ta panta) are created in and through the eternal Word. Creation is from, through and to God – who is the fulness and origin of all love, mercy, righteousness, beauty, language, glory, abundance, "the fountain of all good" (art. 1, Dutch Confession). If we look in the direction of God's revelation-in-time, then God's fulness "unfolds" in His forgiving mercy, punishing righteousness and teaching guidance, for example. In an historical sense we can rightly speak of something new, of a supplementation of "unheard of things." These lie in the extension of what was revealed, even before the fall, of the fulness and unity of God's *revelation* in the works and words of God in time.

The Revelation of Creation, Including Word-Revelation, Remains Universal

A conscious effort has been made to rise above the duality of word and work by using the phrase *revelation of creation*. God's creational work was *creative* speech, and His words were working words. God did not create "out of nothing" but out of Himself, by His commands. He called into existence ("being") and continuance, and He revealed His will as the life-law for creation.

Another element belongs to the life-law in the diversity of the creational order: the law of that special human function which was later distinguished by theoretical analysis in its simplicity as "pistis," religious *believing* as a mode of being and experiencing. Here Reformational theology still stands in opposition to Roman Catholic theology. The anthropological and philosophical "floor" of both faiths contradict each other.

According to the biblical creation-idea, man is not altogether human without faith, and faith is no supernatural gift ("donum superadditum"). Without faith, man has no "complete" human nature. Faith is only a gift of grace when "natural" faith again becomes *really* natural, i.e., *when* the only true God, who revealed Himself in the Word, is *truly* believed and loved, served and honoured.

Supernatural theology is therefore just as unnatural as the "natural" theology, which claims that man can rationally prove God's existence and that without

79

faith in God nobody prospers. God's revelation of grace lies in the extension of His revelation of creation. But He calls for a *radical change* of direction ("conversion") in man's knowledge of God, which was tainted by sin. The revelation of creation itself is dynamically directed to the unfolding and fulfilment of God's love. And this love has existed from eternity and reveals itself in our own perverted time in forgiving grace and punishing righteousness.

For this reason, we have trouble with the claimed "particular" character of the "special" revelation. It is not "special," because it is Word-revelation, nor does it (in an historical sense) bring something "new." Special revelation is special because it reveals that God fulfils His intention as Creator in spite of the fall. Therefore, this revelation refers specially to the work of redemption, the redemption and liberation of created life, so that life can be set straight in its orientation and alignment to the life-law from creation. This life-law is in fact directed to, and liberated by, the unfolding in the *historical* process of the fulfilment of God's kingly rule of love.

Therefore, we do not particularly insist on using the term "special revelation," certainly not when it is not taken as being *one* in Christ with the so-called general revelation. In this context, special revelation would be seen to be historically an extension or supplementation, or rather an unfolding of general revelation in the total order of the revelation of creation.

"Special" in the sense of "particular" has a different meaning. We object to this use, because the meaning of "special" does not do justice to God's universal intention of salvation, which is *normative* for all people. Theologically this idea can perhaps be formulated better as *the universal law-character of the Gospel*.[24] If, as is customary, we see the Gospel as the "special" or "particular" revelation par excellence of the salvation of God, then we must say that God in fact directs Himself in this to all people. On this revelation is also founded the "missionary command" of Matthew 28. This gospel should be believed. This is God's will. This will of God historically became flesh and blood in Christ and in His preaching, but it also became a book in the Holy Scriptures. The human faith-function has to direct and orient itself to this central element if faith is to develop normally and we are to *manifest this Gospel in our temporary life*.

The Achilles heel of theological orthodoxy has always been "ethics." With regard to the remaining, non-pistically qualified life, faith is made independent and is sometimes even absolutized. Viewed philosophically (and philosophy remains the floor on which all theology rests), the faith-function is built into the totality of life by the creational order both as the *function which determines the direction* and as

---

24. Even K. Barth is not always consistent in his sharp dualism of gospel and law. So, for example KD II, 2 p. 619. The gospel is also law "sofern (?, A. T.) es die Form eines an uns gerichteten Anspruchs hat." We ask: When will it not be the case? Does not this depend on a verbal form?

a "limiting-function." The revelation of God that entered history on its pistic law-side is and remains as *universally and generally valid* as the will of God in every other aspect of life. The revelation of creation remains universal, and remains revelation of God in, for and by the creatures in "nature and history."

The revelation of creation is not isolated work-revelation nor word-revelation. As Word-revelation it stands in the centre of creation, because fundamentally it is the Eternal Word of God, Jesus Christ, in Whom the Triune God created and re-creates the cosmos. Creation revelation affects man in the heart of his existence, while the *human reaction* manifests itself *primarily* in the modality of faith. All other modalities – such as logical distinction, conceptualisation, verbal expression and the confessional forming of symbols – are structurally presupposed and built into actual faith. But faith is not tantamount to *one* of its retrocipations and cannot be reduced to one of them.

Why This Treatise?

The practice of science has its own internal meaning. Science is a human task which naturally cannot be isolated in human life and society. Therefore, we oppose the current tendency to *measure* pragmatically the meaning of research by its inherent "social relevancy" or "use" in a certain period. Love, art production and enjoyment, public worship of the church, the production and consumption of goods, sports and many other expressions of life all have their own

82

internal meaning, and do not *only* "derive" their meaning "from a greater totality" (Kuitert). Similarly, the practice of science is a meaningful part of human life (in the case of philosophy and theology, even apart from their inherent "social relevancy").

Science offers its own internal satisfaction and troubles. For these we should praise God, who is the first and last human aim of life.

Moreover, the *interlaced coherence* of science with many other life sectors can be analysed theoretically. In the foreground is the central meaning of theology for ecclesiastical and religious life, and philosophy for the practice of special sciences. It is in this cadre that I should like to offer some remarks about the intention of this text.

What remains now is an objective question. Has theology profited from abandoning the distinction between general and special revelation, which I have advocated here? It is possible that, owing to the high level of abstraction in the present discussion, someone might ask whether it matters when one speaks of the revelation of creation and Word-revelation, or the universal and particular sides of God's self-revelation. Could these issues be more than a mere terminological dispute?

No, that is certainly not the case. The *history* of theology illustrates the *religio-ethical foundation of the opposed distinction* in the pre-Christian, especially Greek, notion of life much better than I have done in this brief chapter. The internal tension, motivated by what Nietzsche signalled as the tragedy of the religious conflict between the Apollonian and the Dionysian, brought about a deep split in Greek thought.

As a result, this dialectic was taken up in Christian life and thought in a transposed form. Theologically it took shape in the double dialectic of an impossible synthesis between Christian life and thought, and an already dialectical "general human" life, which finds itself in the tension of perishable matter and immortal form. This so-called Christian synthesis obtained its classic shape in the theoretical thought-scheme of "nature and grace," which, owning to its *religious depth-dimension*, cannot be bridged monistically by any *theoretical* construction.

In this regard we might look at the work of Hans Schulze in the *Zweidimensionalität der Christlichen Existenz (Dual-Dimensionality of Christian Existence)*. He sees the eschatological and social way of existence bridged in the *personality* of a Christian. Here is an example of the current personalistic construction in which an effort is made to conquer the nature-grace dualism.

Schulze's approach makes Christianity of all confessions – both orthodox and modernistic – in principle defenceless when opposed, for example, by the socialistic view of society. Through a direct evangelical appeal of the Bible to the conscience of the non-academic Christian folk, testimonies of faith concerning such revealed norms as peace, righteousness, freedom, and fraternity are offered as *political* directives. But these testimonies of faith are in no way made concrete in a political sense. Because such testimonies are, in general, valid and accepted principles of the revelation of creation, many people are swayed by these arguments, just as they are swayed by the power of political propaganda. Under this pretext, the fundamental social principle of sovereignty in the own orbit (the responsibility of different social communities) is rejected in Holland as an "empty box." As a result, the so-called "own way" of Christian politics has now become a half-hearted middle position with a tendency to the left, with internally opposing "wings."

This problem is the basis for the permanent question for practical life concerning the way "von der Bibel zur Welt" (from the Bible to the world). The doctrine of "general revelation" paved the way for both the *recognition* and the *denial* in every sense of the revelation of creation. This recognition is especially found in the Roman Catholic traditions of the inborn "moral natural right," which was severed by many humanistic philosophers from its connection to Christian faith and was *taken over as such*.

The denial of the revelation of creation is found in the Protestant accommodation of natural-right traditions (scholastic and humanistic). These we see on the one hand in a minimal, sterile, almost pro-forma, recognised doctrine of a "general revelation." In this the practical meaning almost falls away because of the predominant accent on the "sola Scriptura" as a positivistically manipulated canon even for "ethics." And on the other hand, we see the Protestant accommodation of the periodic, dialectical somersaults. These come about as a result of the undue accent on the natural, general, and universal acts of revelation of God in the *history* of humanity.

In the case of ethics this involves the well-known split between *philosophical ethics*, which by its nature is not Christian but can only be "speculative" or "rational" and theological ethics. The latter, in spite of all exegetical differences, is considered to stand on the solid ground of the "data" of Word-revelation.

My alternative here is evident.[25] I oppose the meaning traditionally given to ethics, namely as a "prescriptive" or "normative" leading instance to life – theological ethics for Christians, and philosophical ethics for non- or semi-Christians or for the "natural" life of Christians. I believe human actions are only led in part, and never decisively, by "ethics," nor by any other *science*. Religion and faith are the guiding principles which tip the scale. This claim is universally valid. Anthropologically it revolves around a basic motivation, an "ethos."

In the elaboration of this thought, the idea of a Christian science (philosophy and special sciences) plays the part traditionally attributed to theological ethics. In philosophical anthropology and

25. Cf. among others in *Philosophia Reformata* my contribution "Christian Alternatives for Traditional Ethics," in Vol. 38 (1973) pp. 167-177.

the doctrine of praxis (inspired by Dooyeweerd's doctrine of ground-motives and his conception of time), we discovered the depth dimension of the *ethos* as a datum taking up an important part of what one might call the field of "philosophical ethics." Here the continuity with traditional philosophical ethics is also maintained (Cf. Chapter 9).

Lastly, I should like to turn to the issue of terminological relevancy. Naturally tolerance, souplesse and an understanding of intentions must be taken into account. A consistent use of the current distinction between general and special revelation can easily camouflage deep differences in the objective insights and in the total view of reality which is at stake here. Such use can delay the true reformation of thought. Let me illustrate this point with two experiments. If I make use of the current terminology, we might be led to make unacceptable pronouncements:

1) The biblical Word-revelation is an integral part of and is taken up into the whole of the all-determining revelation of creation. But if I say that "special" revelation forms a part of "general" revelation, such a formulation would be theologically unacceptable.

2) Word-revelation is just as universal and generally valid as the revelation of creation. But if I should say that the "special," "particular" revelation is just as universal as the "general" revelation of God, then I would commit a

theological error.

In the biblical, ecclesiastical, and theological usage, the term, "special" revelation could rather be replaced theologically by expressions such as rebirth, enlightenment by the Holy Spirit, the breaking through of a spiritually renewed insight, the opening of the eyes of the heart, etc. The old theologians, including Calvin, spoke of Word-revelation "cum affectu et effectu." But this definition is inadequate because it can also be used to describe "general revelation," even though "affect" and "effect" according to Romans 1 refers to an extra hardening of one's heart.

Terminological issues should not be overestimated, yet they often point us to deeper problems at hand. The terminological issues are not as simple as they might appear. In the light of our discussion, Reformational terms – "Sola Scriptura" and "Sola Fide" – are to a certain extent liberated from hypostatisation or even absolutization. They keep their inspiring central meaning in the conflict against Rome. A truly radical elaboration of this principle must oppose the very life that feeds these expressions, because the "Scriptura" itself teaches that it cannot exist "Sola" and it may not be elevated to the whole of God's self-revelation. Similarly, "fides" itself does not exist "Sola." *According to creation*, fides has its inner coherence in breadth (modally and typically) and in depth (dispositionally and ethically) with love, justice, language, the power of discrimination, etc.

88

Moreover, faith is not *exclusively* directed to the Scriptures and does not receive all its norms from this source. The law-of-faith, the revelation of God in time, also takes shape in what *happens* historically, economically, aesthetically, juridically, socially, and morally. Here we traditionally refer to God's general revelation in nature and history, on which theology preferably does not say too much, with the exception of Marxist theology.

Thus from the traditional scheme of general and special revelation, in the more orthodox theology, the general revelation becomes hollow and sterile. But in the opening-up direction of the cosmic law-order of the aspects of reality themselves lies the normative indication for concrete life. By this we judge whether reality is directed transcendentally to its Origin and Destination. The words of the Catechism of Heidelberg summarise this opening-up direction quite simply: from a real faith, according to God's law and to God's honour.[26]

---

26. Cf. H. Dooyeweerd, "Maatstaven ter onderkenning van progressieve en reactionaire bewegingen in de historische ontwikkeling," in: Jaarboek Kon. Ned. Ac. van Wetensch., 1958.

CHAPTER 3

Individual and Social Ethics

Introduction

I WOULD NOW like to discuss the nature and task of ethics, its place in human life, and its role in scientific activity. Special attention will be given to the distinction intended in the words "individual" and "social" as they relate to ethics.

It is not possible to offer a broad discussion of concrete issues in personal and societal life. What I am attempting is an initial Christian self-investigation on the part of the moral philosopher – a self-investigation of his task, of the significance of ethics for Christian life, and of the method of ethics.

The terms "ethics," "social ethics," and "Christian ethics" are often used in everyday language. In academic circles the distinction between "theological ethics" and "philosophical ethics" is also well known. Everyone knows that these terms have something to do with norms, values, and laws, as well as with feelings, customs, social structures, and religious convictions. Most of us expect that ethics will give us guidance, or at least indications of how to make decisions about the various problems of practical life. For this reason, ethics is supposed to be a "practical" science which tells us what is good and what is not good.

The common understanding of ethics described above must be discussed further. For the sake of this argument, we shall grant that ethics is a "practical" science. We then need to ask if science should be regarded as the guide to life. If we say that science should be regarded this way, then we may be discriminating against the simple believer who has never studied ethics and perhaps does not even know what ethics means. He knows that the Bible says he needs the guidance of the Holy Spirit and the teaching of Scriptures. He knows that he needs wisdom, peace, patience, frankness, insight, and a number of other virtues. And he acknowledges that he does not possess these virtues but needs to receive them by prayer. In this way he knows that Christian life, in principle, is possible because he believes the message of the Scriptures: in Christ he has received wisdom, righteousness, redemption and sanctification as well (1 Cor. 1:30-31).

If this is the case, then why and from what source does "ethics" enter our life?

"Philosophia Dux Vitae" (Cicero)

In the ancient Greek culture of the fifth and sixth centuries before Christ, the old pagan religions were declining. At the same time a struggle was taking place between the two major types of religion: the primitive nature-religions and the culture-religions whose ruined sanctuaries can still be seen today. Both these types of religion were undergoing a process of secularisation and were losing their grip on practical life.

As their culture evolved, the Greeks developed, for the first time in world history, the method of scientific thought. The transition from practical, religion-guided views of life and death, and of origin and destiny in personal and societal life, took place in "philosophy." Philosophy even substituted for the old-fashioned beliefs in gods and spirits.

But it was not long before philosophy itself became more "practical." In the history of philosophy there have been several long periods in which a particular theme of philosophy, namely ethics, was predominant. Well known among these periods was the "Hellenistic" age, which, roughly speaking, extended from 300 B.C. to 300 A.D.

During that time, philosophers tried to take over the complete guidance of life. Cicero, a very popular philosopher who had great oratorical talent, offered his famous praise of philosophy in the words "O philosophia dux vitae" – "O philosophy, guide to life." By this he meant the rational, scientific guide to life.

What happened when Christianity entered this world of heathen culture? As mentioned in chapter 1, the first theologian to write a book about theological ethics was Ambrose. He imitated Cicero to a large extent by giving his work on ethics the title: *Three Books on the Duties of the Clergyman*. This book was very similar to Cicero's work on ethics entitled *De Officiis (On Duties)*.

A comparison of the contents of these two books on ethics shows that Ambrose largely agreed with Cicero and wanted to supplement rather than oppose or change Cicero's ethics. He added to Cicero by saying that those who were clergymen should obey the moral rules more than ordinary Christians. In addition, clergymen were called to obey additional stricter rules than ordinary Christians. In this way he borrowed from Cicero the distinction between ordinary duties and what were called "perfect duties." This distinction has had a tremendous influence on theology. In particular, it inspired the monastic life and the doctrine relating to it.

I shall briefly mention only two other well-known Christian theologians, Boethius and Thomas Aquinas. Boethius was in prison when he wrote his famous *De Consolatione Philosophiae (On the Consolations of Philosophy)*. It is significant that this famous scholar found his consolation in his difficult circumstances through philosophical science rather than from the Word of God.

The other theologian worth noting here is Thomas Aquinas. On questions of ethics he has had an enormous influence on theology, including Protestant theology, right up to the present day.

Aquinas combined philosophical ethics, which he regarded as social ethics, with theological ethics, which he viewed as individual ethics.

The Overrating of Ethics

Before we discuss the distinction between individual and social ethics, we must realise that our Western culture has great expectations of ethics. People have lost their confidence in the Bible and in the guidance of the Holy Spirit. Instead, they try to displace God's guide by the guide offered by science, whether that guide is seen to be philosophical or theological ethics, social or personal ethics.

Although scientific investigation is necessary, we must always keep in mind that it is a form of human activity that is not guided by logic alone. Logic does not even take the first place in guiding the sciences. Science, like all human activity, is guided by a spiritual power – either the power of God through his Word and Spirit, or in apostasy by the humanistic spiritual power. For this reason, we need a Christian approach in the sciences. A Christian way of scientific investigation and explanation is not the same as a theological or ethical approach. I shall return to this point later.

For the present I would offer two remarks. We are not permitted to make substitutes for the guidance of God through his Word and Spirit. I am referring here to the guidance of any science, whether it be economics, jurisprudence, sociology, psychology, philosophy, or theology. To do this would demonstrate typical Western pride.

Second, so far as we need scientific help in the various issues of modern life, we need Christian sciences, re-formed sciences. We need these perspectives because all the contemporary sciences are dominated by humanistic views of life and society, and by the humanistic belief in the necessity of guidance by neutral, purely logical science. The existence of such a neutral science is dogmatically presupposed.

Re-Formation of Science Begins with Philosophy

To this point I have been trying to say something about the general place of science, and particularly of ethics, in human life as a whole. I have concluded that it is not science but the spiritual power of God through his Word and Spirit that provides guidance for human life. Conversely, in apostasy it is the humanistic spiritual power that provides guidance for life.

In the case of the humanistic spiritual power in Western culture, the religious apostasy has often concealed itself by proclaiming that an autonomous reason can provide guidance for life through scientific thinking. The dangers and temptations of this Western apostasy have continually been exerting an influence on Christian life. The imitation of pagan philosophy by Christian theology, or at least the blending of

Christian theology with non-Christian philosophical patterns of thought, have had a harmful effect on Christian belief and Christian life.

Through God's grace a reformational movement within Christendom occurred during the 16th century. Guided by the Holy Spirit rather than theology, Christian belief could make a new beginning by returning to the Scriptures. In this return Christians were helped and sustained by theologians such as Calvin and Luther. This Reformation was not an isolated historical event but was a continuing process.

In the further development of this process during the first quarter of the twentieth century, a reformational and biblical breakthrough occurred in the field of scientific thought. This breakthrough was evident first in the acceptance of philosophy as a foundational science, structurally implicit in every special science, including theology. The deepest and most general concepts, patterns, and methods of thinking are discussed and developed in philosophy according to the law of God for scientific thought. This law of God for science includes the laws of logic, as everybody knows, but it goes far beyond logic. The law of God includes the normative structure for the whole task of scientific thought.

It is against this background that we investigate the place, task, and practical significance of many kinds of ethics.

Individual Ethics

My first statement on this subject is deliberately formulated in a provocative manner: the distinction between individual and social ethics makes little sense. Let me try to explain this statement. Obviously, the distinction relates to personal life on the one hand, and social life on the other. But what is personal life? It cannot be set in opposition to, or separated from, social life. In social life we are also acting personally.

In every area of social life we are personally responsible to God and to our fellow men in the situation in which we are acting. Our situations and circumstances always and everywhere include relations with God and our fellow men. Even in what might be regarded as a strictly personal matter, such as enjoying a personal hobby as an amateur photographer, or our personal health and hygiene, we are not acting strictly as isolated individuals. Our handling of these situations is determined by cultural (that is by social) patterns and possibilities. Yet the way we handle them is also influenced by personal style, personal gifts, personal character and qualities.

Theoretically speaking, if scientific aid is needed at all in this area of life, a place for personal ethics may be possible only in the field of such virtues as neatness, attachment to the environment in which we are raised, love for plants and pets, etc. But the vast majority of personal virtues and vices are as much social as personal. Human life, in fact, is always personal, but it is nearly always social as well. Far more important than personal ethics, therefore, is social ethics, supposing that ethics is the correct word for what we have in mind.

What Is Social Ethics?

In everyday language, ethics does not always refer to a science. Very often it is used to describe a way of life or a life-style. Sometimes it refers simply to an attitude, a mentality, or a custom. In this case ethics is something like morals.

This non-theoretical use of the term "social ethics" may be accepted in everyday language, but "social ethics" has an additional, scientific sense. It describes a particular kind of scientific activity. What is the place and task of this science? Is social ethics (in this theoretical and scientific sense) the science that should give us the correct insight into what is wrong and what is good for society? This question cannot be answered with a simple yes or no. The issues involved – society, insight, right and wrong – are complex.

We can certainly take as our point of contact with current thinking the insight that social ethics has to do with questions of norms, values, traditions, and structures in social life. But as soon as someone versed in ethics deals with a particular issue in society, it becomes clear that he is dealing with a question on which some other science, and sometimes two or three other sciences, are more competent to speak. Then a central question arises. What is the special task of the practitioner of ethics? What is his particular expertise?

If we say that this task is to deal with questions of right and wrong, good and evil, we find that many lawyers, politicians, economists and even artists may disagree. In their consideration of questions of right and wrong or good and evil in their particular fields, they have no intention of accepting the guidance of ethics. In a more or less friendly way, they simply let the philosophers and theologians go on talking about ethical questions while they get on with the business of deciding the issues of right and wrong, good and evil in their particular field. In my opinion they are quite right in doing so. Neither philosophers nor theologians are experts in the special fields mentioned above. In all of these realms we encounter questions of right and wrong, good and evil, but we rightly do not deal with all these issues in terms of ethical questions.

Ethics as a Special Science

Here I would only make one exception. This would be for the counsellors dealing with the problems of marriage, family, and friendship, particularly in matters of sexuality, although not exclusively. These problems have always been considered ethical questions and are today often regarded incorrectly as merely psychological problems. These are the questions that may be allotted to ethics as a special science.

Ethics in this sense may be very helpful in practical problems when something goes wrong in marriage, in relations between parents and children, in questions of homosexuality, divorce and the like. In passing, I point out that these private or personal problems are also social problems. They are private or personal only from the point of view of other societal forms such as the state, church, business enterprise, trade union or football club, for example. But they are social problems in that they occur in social structures of human life other than those just mentioned.

We shall now try to formulate a strict definition of ethics as a special science. *Ethics as a special science deals with questions in those areas of life that are qualified by love in its typical societal forms: love in marriage, family and friendship.*

Can "Social Ethics" Be Abolished?

Evidently, we *could* use ethics as a special science relating to the fairly small field of the societal forms qualified by love. But what are we to do with the old pretensions of philosophical and/or theological ethics? As I have pointed out, there are many practical problems in modern society. To deal with these issues we usually call on the scientific aid of experts in the particular sciences (and for good reasons), rather than the aid of philosophers and theologians practising ethics. Can we therefore abolish "social ethics," philosophical ethics and theological ethics?

In recent times, philosophers and social scientists have been compelled to undertake a thorough self-examination. (Part of the motivation for this has been the influence of Marxism.) In all their fields of study, a stormy battle over methodology has raged. The fighting has been particularly fierce during the turbulent decade of the sixties.

Scientists and scholars, especially those in the humanities, should be commended for examining their place and task and, not the least, the meaning and significance of their studies for the realm of practical life. The self-evident nature of their guiding role in human life can no longer be taken for granted in modern social sciences. So in contemporary thinking we can see a return to philosophical ethics. But what is the reason for this return?

Philosophical Ethics Makes a Comeback

Both the old and the new rationalistic positivism has been a willing instrument of several ideologies. Both Marxism and capitalism can and do use it to their advantage. Since rationalistic positivism is supposed to be nothing more than a neutral logical instrument, it can be easily built into every theology. Orthodox theologians all over the world are even using it, often quite subconsciously, as a logical method in dogmatics.

But Marxist philosophers in particular have become aware of this situation, and they have tried to overcome it by promoting philosophical ethics. Once again, we return to scientific ethics.

In this modern form the old pretensions of philosophical ethics return. Philosophers adopt the religious pretension of being able to provide a scientific aid and guidance to practical life. They posit a utopian framework in which the whole society must be developed.

In fact, this aid and guidance is not merely scientific. It also embodies the power of humanistic religion, which believes in the guidance of human life by scientific reason and scientific, logical methods. The old Western apostasy of the deification of reason has returned, in spite of all the deceptions and failures of that apostasy found in Western cultural and ecclesiastical history.

The Inherent Problem of Theological Ethics

As suggested earlier, Christianity, today, as in every age, tends to adapt and accommodate itself to the patterns of life and thought which are current in the non-Christian world. This accommodation also occurs in theology and particularly in theological ethics.

Operating within the old scheme of nature and supernature, ethics often deals with "natural problems" by following uncritically the related "neutral" sciences. But contemporary ethics claims, in exactly the same way as medieval ethics, to be able to provide the necessary supernatural complement in the way of biblical insights, biblical concepts and indications.

This old and recurring mixture of possibly genuine biblical theology with rationalistic methods makes Christianity very weak. Christianity is now left without almost any firm resistance to Marxism and modernism in theology. Over the last 25 years I have seen many very conservative Reformed theologians who have believed more in their confession perhaps, rather than confessing their belief. As a result, they have lost their orthodox theology, sometimes within just a few years.

In most cases I suspect ethics has been the stone that has caused theological orthodoxy to collapse like a house of cards. Perhaps I should say: like a house of cards built upon the sand of human reasoning. "And great was the fall thereof." As a result, many Christians and many ministers have become so afraid of any renewal that they close their eyes and minds to the extreme urgency of a Reformational renewal of the sciences in general, including orthodox theology.

Alternatives to Traditional Ethics

In the context of the provisional system of a biblical reformational philosophy, we should now reconsider the function of traditional ethics, whether it is called theological or philosophical. My provisional theory on this issue is outlined very briefly in the following paragraphs.

i) No human science or theory is foundational for Christian life. The only foundation for Christian life is a regenerate heart and a biblical belief manifesting itself in a Christian attitude to life ("ethos"). Philosophically speaking, the same holds true in the structural realm for every human being. Foundational for all human life is the religious direction and choice of the heart, which is demonstrated in the case of persons without Christian faith in apostate or humanistic (un)belief.

ii) A number of special sciences, usually called "humanities" or "behavioural sciences," have the task of enlightening and advising us in the related fields of practical life. I am referring to instances in which the specific problems are qualified as juridical, political, economic, social, logical, historical, technical, aesthetic, ecclesiastical, etc.

iii) In accordance with the inner nature of science (i.e., in accordance with the law of God given in the inner structure of scientific thought), every special science has within itself the indwelling power of fundamental philosophical ideas. These are in relation to their own particular basic ideas. From the Christian point of view, these sciences should be internally renewed by a genuinely Christian scientific approach, the foundation for which is provided in a Reformed philosophy.

iv) The distinction between individual and social ethics and science is almost entirely without practical significance. All the sciences relating to human behaviour are, as a matter of fact, ways of dealing with human relations. That is, they are social in character. Even psychology, education, theology, and psychiatry, when they are person-centred, can never properly isolate the person from his relations with his fellow man. Remember the central commandment of love, in which love for God is inseparably connected with love of our neighbours (Mt. 22:30-40).

v) Among the special sciences there is a need for one special science that is neither philosophy nor theology. This special science could be called "ethics as a special science." The problems of love and sex, which in the past have been a major part of ethics (whether Christian ethics or not), may be assigned to this special science of love. This should not be confused with the sciences auxiliary to it such as psychology, psychiatry, theology, etc. The special science of love has a particular field and particular methods not reducible to other fields and other methods.

Traditional Ethics in "Social Ethics"

A random selection of topics generally treated in "social ethics" includes the ethics of work, industrial enterprise, politics, juridical punishment, educational punishment, developmental aid, environmental care, art, war, traffic, and bioethics. And these are only a few of the topics. I have a list of more than 20 types of ethics altogether, gathered from the literature in my field of study.

Most of these contributions to ethics have been written by theologians, especially those from churches associated with the World Council of Churches. The old confusion of Christianity with a moral system is still very much alive in those circles.

But we must admit that modern theology is dealing

106

(often in a misguided fashion) with the burning issues of our world. It deals with problems which we, as Christians, may not deny. In more orthodox churches these problems are often merely mentioned in passing without being treated seriously. Sermons dealing with practical life are generally limited to prayer and the development of personal virtues.

Such sermons may have their place, but this limitation in the realm of preaching will only strengthen the misconception that Christianity is a system of personal morals. It will also strengthen the misunderstanding that societal problems can be solved by personal morality, a message that modern personalistic philosophy is also preaching! We should take note of the almost religious praise of psychology in the theological training of ministers in many modern churches.

At the same time, I do not plead for sermons dealing with the social, political, economic and related problems of today's world. We, as theologians and as philosophers, need to be more careful and modest.

It seems obvious that the kind of topics mentioned above require a range of insights of a special scientific character. These must first of all be provided by scientists in each of the special fields or, in the case of politics for example, by skilled politicians experienced in the particular field. We who are philosophers and theologians first and foremost should not deal with these complicated questions in which we are not experts. Practical experience, responsibility and scientific expertise cannot be replaced by theology or prophetic sermons. On the other hand, gospel preaching and theology cannot be replaced by philosophy.

The Roman Catholic tradition may claim that the Pope and the theological and philosophical teachers of the church are the only experts in the field of knowing God's will for the whole of human life. But, in the light of Reformational insights, this cannot be true. Such a monopoly of church leaders, theologians and philosophers does not exist.

CHAPTER 4

Structural Sources of Social Criticism

The Deepest Levels of Social Criticism

IF THE TASK of our social criticism is to be delimited more closely, we should start by indicating the deepest level of our life: the dimension in which all questions, including social ones, converge at a focal point. At first glance this approach does not offer a new insight for Christians. In and through faith we know that the world's *burden of sin* truly lies "at the bottom of all questions."

Professing Christians have always known this fact, and from this point of view they have always exercised social criticism, even when their faith degenerated. Even during the early centuries we witness such criticism by the apostolic fathers, the apologists and the church fathers. The oldest example of post-biblical Christian criticism of society in a truly magnificent style is found in the "De Civitate Dei" of St. Augustine. The contributions of Luther and Calvin belong to the same category. Today we

109

differentiate more clearly between wrong factual *conditions* and wrong *structures* that lie at the bottom of these conditions, although this conviction is too vague to be absolutely correct. In general, the causes of deplorable situations in human existence are now thought to be *deeper* than the sphere of direct causes and factual circumstances. Here, "deeper" implies more than the individual human character.

Christian criticism of society has always offered insight into deeper and more spiritual dimensions in social structures. We have already mentioned the traditional understanding of our "burden of sin." In the biblical understanding of this phrase, the notions of solidarity ("everyone has sinned . . ." – Romans 3:23) and judgement ("the wrath of God is revealed . . ." – Romans 1:18) abound. But it is difficult to explain the *structural relations* between this depth-dimension of sin and judgement on the one hand, and the factual needs and distress on the other.

Before discussing this serious defect in the Christian criticism of society, I should like to look more closely at the first and deepest criticism. This criticism tries to designate the ultimate grounds and deepest reasons for all the misery of humanity. This issue does not only concern Christians. But the sharpest and deepest criticism of society can be designated and confessed only by Christianity. Humanity and its societal forms are related to the person and will of God as the creator who "a priori" is not guilty of our misery, but imputes to us our misery . . . the consequences of punishment for our burden of sin (Amos 3:6). We must remember, however, that non-Christians also penetrate to the deepest level of *their* criticism of society. Perhaps I shall be contradicted on this point by those who say that only pious Christians attain this depth in their criticism of society. Regarding the contents of this depth, this observation is indeed true.

If, however, we want to discuss man (anthropology) and society (social philosophy) in the light of a Christian scientific approach then we must also consider the depth-*structures* of man and society. (Here I omit the subjective factual side and contents: the Christian confession.) Non-Christians also express their structurally essential "last" word, their "deepest" conviction, their "eventual" basis of explanation of what is actually the deepest dimension of society. They, too, as human beings would not be able to shun the central questions and problems and would have to answer them with their subjective contents. One seeks *the meaning of life* in the same place one finds the central source for social criticism.

Happiness as the Meaning of Life?

Since ancient times, man has tried to find the meaning of life in the realm of human happiness. This realm has been the most essential, deepest, highest, and ultimate end of all aspirations. In essence, everyone will assent to this goal, Christians included. But a Christian also considers everything in the context of

111

the biblical words "salvation" and "blessedness" (re-instated love-community with God and man, shalom, etc.), whereas non-Christians criticize society differently and have manifold answers which change in the course of time.

Naturally one is soon forced to describe happiness with adjectives such as *highest*, *greatest* and the like. Sensual pleasure counts as the highest happiness for many, soon supplemented or even replaced by "spiritual" pleasure in the sense of cultural enjoyment. Originally many saw the highest happiness in "freedom," the magic word that originally meant "the safe security of feeling at home in one's sphere." Later, freedom came to mean political freedom (as opposed to the lack of rights of strangers and slaves); then it evolved into "inner freedom," as opposed to the external circumstances of an economical, political, or corporeal nature.

All these variations were already evident before our Christian era. Christ Himself spoke about being "truly" free, indicating that even then the term "free" must have had various dimensions and false meanings. Apart from lust, pleasure, and freedom (and all three in many variations), reason was added as the highest, deepest, and last refuge of humanity. Later, utility was added. Today there are many formulations, such as peace, freedom, prosperity, justice, liveable circumstances, humanitarianism, solidarity, and so forth.

In every age, criticism of society has its *starting point*, consciously or unconsciously, in the answers to the last and deepest questions of society. Yet even when one wants to "put aside" all faith or religiousness, it *is not* cancelled out. According to creation, this is structurally impossible. From an anthropological and social philosophical point of view, human society has in "society," once and for all, the spiritual depth-dimensions from which a human being, a social form, a society, and all humanity *lives*, *thinks* and *criticizes*.

The "Ethos" as Depth Level of Life

The term that is used frequently to describe this "attitude of life," "focus of life," and "spiritual attitude" seems to be the word "ethos." In Dooyeweerd's terms, one would be able to discuss the dialectical dynamics of a religious ground motive, which dominates the life *and* thought of a series of generations in a certain cultural sphere. The philosophical difference in nuance between "ethos" and "ground motive" can be left aside here. What we have been concerned with until now is the beginning of an answer to the question laid before us: *whence* the criticism of society in our times?

I have tried to build up the answer from a systematic, philosophical viewpoint. Hence, an important distinction must be made. I have tried to show the "whence" as a spiritual depth-level; being human, and thus being fellow-man in a society, should be differentiated from various structures and conditions which lie nearer the surface. To indicate the depth-level I have used the term "ethos." Strictly speaking, this is not the ultimate word. In the ethos there exists another spiritual "centre" that cannot be defined, but which can be discussed. Considering the individual human being, the term "heart" (or soul or spirit) can be used here. The Holy Scriptures say that from the heart flow the springs of life; the heart of man is unfathomably deep and cannot easily be understood. In the heart of man the deepest decisions are taken.

However, in the focal point of his existence, man is not a human being on his own; he is part of the spiritual community, which in turn has a head, centre, or root. In the central fulness of his existence, man has a share in Christ and His body through the Holy Ghost and through faith. If this is not the case, then he is nevertheless in a spiritual community, namely the kingdom of Satan, the sinful world, being human and of the world. Strictly speaking, nothing scientific can be said about this, nor anything "theological" either. Only through Christian faith are we aware of these common human possibilities, which are realities of spiritual nature. Non-Christians know this element too, but misinterpret it as "the family of man," for example, or "universal humanity."

Here, in the religious centre of the spiritual radical unity, we see the actual starting point of our human life and society, as well as our reflection on it. No human judgement can be passed on this fact, and no scientific analysis can be made. It is accessible only to God's eyes and to some extent to the human eye of faith. In the "ethos," on the other hand, we can note a certain visibility and a larger *differentiation*, which is linked to certain cultures, periods, and developments from which it obtains a closer characterisation. Here we are already in the sphere of temporary structures (philosophically one can also say: time-structures) of human life and society, even if we are speaking of the most slightly differentiated depth-dimension of the typical human act-structure.

Structure as Normative Principle

Finally, in answer to the question about the origin of the criticism of society, we should clarify another misunderstanding common in our subjectivistic age. The subjective (i.e., factual) starting points of human life and criticism have been discussed already. We then indicated that this factual depth-dimension is determined by the structural datum of the human and co-human situation, even though this dimension is realised and experienced in both a Christian and non-Christian way. In our subjectivistic climate of thought, which has been dominant since the Renaissance, the term "structure" has usually been understood subjectivistically as only an historically developed, purely human datum, acquirement or formation.

Anyone who adopts this point of view would most certainly misunderstand the preceding discussion. "Structure," as designated above, is meant primarily as *normative principle* (law). In our human and fellow-human situation we are under the religious law of revelation and concentration, which totally determines our lives in its various depth-levels both normatively and dynamically. This law is an incentive to the unfolding of potentialities. It leads to self-reflection and self-knowledge, in order to *profess*, in our ultimate concentration, the final word and answer to the last and deepest question.

This final answer of our heart is governed by the commandment of God: "My son, give me your heart." This starting point of our life, thoughts, society, etc., stands under the double commandment of love in its well known, irreversible order and equivalence: the love of God and our neighbour as ourselves. On these two commandments depend the whole law and the prophets.

With these last words we arrive at the end of this lengthy and important answer to the question of the origin of all social criticism. In what follows, the meaning will become clearer, and each stage in the argument can be carefully followed.

The Bible as Source

"The whole law and the prophets" – this is a set expression for all the writings of the Old Testament, not only the "prescriptions, commandments and ordinations" but also the history and the accounts of God's deeds, the whole revelation of God and His will. The story of creation, the history that tells us how God's creative command "called" everything into being from nothing and gave it its own character and law of life, is also understood under the "law and prophets." All of this depends on the double law of love, not in the sense that the fulfilment of love is the law, but that the fulfilment of the *commandment* is love.

This is of the greatest importance to social life. We can neither discuss nor criticize society in a serious, Christian manner if our faith in creation remains non-active. Christians, however sincere in their faith, do not automatically live and think and criticize in a Christian fashion – certainly not in the case of the problematics of society. In fact, we hardly have a tradition from which we could have learned to act in such a way. The opposite is true, as I will explain presently.

Discussion about "the" Society

Societal life is characterised by an abundance of structural diversity, which is systematically obscured by a kind of levelling talk about "the society" and its "groups." This same levelling is also caused and strengthened by talk about "the reigning class" or about "those in authority in society." Highly educated people have discussions and write books which are advertised in the newspapers under titles such as: "How do we divide power?" "Where is the actual power?" Naturally this concise way of discussing "the" society can be useful and easy. It is sensible to talk and write in *short* sentences, which even in a fleeting encounter will make a lasting impression. Unfortunately, there are dangers attached to such an approach. The danger becomes acute when the "whole" which is denot-

117

ed as "the society" is provided with adjectives and labels. That society soon becomes a capitalist society, a consumption society, a responsible society, a soviet (= council) society, an affluent society, a critical society, etc.

There is a great need for Christians to develop a fundamental criticism about speaking of "the" society. Our criticism must go further and deeper than the appreciable difference of nuance that is implied in the expression "pluralistic society," which would consist of "groups." It is scientifically incorrect and fruitless to discuss "the" society in this way. In essence this usage is scientifically useless, and its use almost inevitably leads to misunderstanding and sometimes far-reaching errors.

In the abundant variety of human life and community, the limitless danger hidden in this usage can cause us to lose sight of the *revelational data* of the creation "according to their kind," *data* that implies an abundance of normativity.

Suffice to say that only in our radically *Christian* creational belief are we to know and fulfil God's will in principle in the diverse "social" sectors of our human community. In essence we are dealing here with the acknowledgement of the unique character and individual responsibility of the distinguishable spheres of life.

This is also a modern scientific issue. In the first place the issue here is wisdom – the knowledge of the world. As the Scriptures teach us, this knowledge may not be associated either exclusively nor automatically with "the fear of the Lord," which is the beginning and principle of true wisdom of life. The Christian believer keeps in mind that God made everything after its own kind and also knows "the time and the way." His *knowledge* of life and the circumstances of his own situation and of his fellow-men, of what to do and what to leave, acquires with prayer and intercession the "real knowledge and all discernment so that you can approve the things that are excellent" (Phil. 1:9-10) in a variety of situations.

In the modern phase of the development of our culture, our wisdom of life does not depend on experience of life only, but on the accompaniment of good or bad sciences as well. Science plays a very important role in our modern lives. It is so extensive that we can overestimate its value and forget that, considered *structurally*, it does not play the most fundamental and decisive, let alone leading, role in human life. It originates from the deeper dimensions of human life as well as community: from the "ethos," but also from "the societal structures."

Two Errors

The sciences render us important services in teaching us to know and to distinguish the unique character of things. From the time of original sin and the total corruption of life, our practical as well as our scientific knowledge of the societal structures has been poor and always susceptible to improvement, and yet such insight

119

cannot be called worthless for a true acquisition of knowledge. The same applies to the object of knowledge – the societal structures and the phenomena themselves.

We must be wary of two errors that are still propagated even by theologians. The first is that, through sin and its results, we can have no certain and trustworthy knowledge about the normative structural principles of human society. The other error is that society itself has now become a purely subjective and arbitrary product of human creativity, so that everything is endlessly changeable. Although these modern (historistic) dogmas in anthropology and the human and societal sciences are now generally acceptable, they are contrary to everybody's experience of life and contrary to the Christian belief in creation.

For every Christian or non-Christian criticism of society, the creational belief connected with a divine order of creation (through which our human life is what it is) takes on great importance. After all, criticism is testing, sifting, separating, judging. Consciously or unconsciously we then use *criteria*, *norms* or at least *norm-principles*. The fact that God gave this normativity in the divine revelation of His Will (revelation of creation) in "Scripture and nature" (Art. 2, Dutch Confession) makes it impossible for every criticism of society, faced with revelation, to choose either a negative or positive position.

A Few Historical Notes

One of the most important principles for the whole of societal life is that of the mutual relationships among the many sectors of human community. Long before our modern era, Europeans had always maintained the idea that the state was regarded as the life-integrating factor, despite cosmopolitan tendencies and remainders of isolating primitivism. Even in the ancient Greek polis-idea, man only became a full human being as a citizen. In both the Spartan aristocracy and the Athenian democracy, the state was the strong totalising and integrating life-connection above the other societal forms in the "holy order" (= hierarchy).

Roman Catholic criticism of society in the Middle Ages preferred *not* to direct itself to the permanent role of the state in the "natural" community. It declared that the kings in their "guiding" reign adapted themselves too little or not at all to ecclesiastical and spiritual interests. Here we see a social criticism that was rather complex, but which, in spite of all its apparently unacceptable tendencies, generally had a sincere concern for the spiritual welfare of the world.

The Lutheran criticism of society does not differ basically from this position. If we read the treatises of Thomas Aquinas, "On the Reign of the Kings," and compare these with Luther's writings, "To the Spiritual Nobility of the German Nation" (1520) and "On the Secular Authorities" (1523), we are struck not only by the resemblance in Christian pastoral concern, but also by the resemblance in the semi-

Christian, semi-pre-Christian ancient view on the life of the state. In spite of errors and later degeneracies, Luther still brought forward important views for a Christian criticism of society, as for example the distinction between office and person. As a result of fundamental defects, this position practically led to the sterilisation of his spiritual and pious criticism of society. This sterility received the notorious form of the double moral: the moral of office and the personal moral.

In the social criticism of Reformed Protestantism, we see a new element gradually emerging. This was the case with Calvin himself, Marnix of St. Aldegonde, and William of Orange. They realized that rulers and authorities had a divine calling in the sphere of life that differed *principally* from the task of ecclesiastical officials. Calvin, more than Luther, improved the climate of thought. But in spite of the murderers of the tyrants ("monarchomachen"), a long time passed before the biblical ideas of Calvin about life on earth acquired the historical maturity that we notice in A. Kuyper's view on social relations.

When Kuyper developed his famous "architectonic" criticism of society, he did not simply criticize the economic and cultural inequality but the whole society. He realised quite clearly the necessity of a conscious view about the character of different societal structures and their mutual relations. From this view he derived a critical criterion by which to test (in principle) the execution of authority by the "officials" in the diverse spheres of life. The point of contact with practice is lacking in Luther's religious view about the structure of authority. This makes it socially sterile and devoid of real criticism. As an exception, Luther once incited the landowners against the emperor, but only when he saw that the emperor could not be personally converted to the faith of the Reformation. This is a completely unacceptable argument.

In 1880, Kuyper formulated the principle of "sovereignty in the individual orbit" for the mutual relations among societal structures. This was a significant development and a deep inspiration to the scientific study of human relations. Unfortunately, Kuyper was not able to elaborate adequately on this principle which could have countered the steadily spreading de-Christianisation of our people and the whole world. Nor could Kuyper's principle resist the penetration from the outside, which gave access to socialist and liberalist thought. Only in the narrow but virile trend of the "Calvinistic Philosophy" was a wider and deeper foundation provided for Christian social criticism. Otherwise, "sovereignty in the individual orbit" did not receive any spectacular publicity, "true to its nature." This social criticism is not revolutionary in the ordinary secular sense, but in the sense in which the Bible speaks of the renewal of our thought through the Holy Spirit, in communion with Christ, through His Spirit and Word.

Whence Social Criticism?

So far, little has been said of Christian social criticism on the surface levels of "society." Only an indication was given of its source, its ethos and its Christian-scientific starting point. In fact, we only touched the issue of its background and its breeding ground. The "whence" of the current social criticism that cannot be called Christian, even if there are valuable elements in it, must still be discussed. The current non-Christian social criticism is apparently and to a great extent always leftist, socialist or (neo-) Marxist.

There is also another social criticism, less noisy but no less deeply rooted in another humanistic type of faith than that of the "leftist" majority. The non-socialistic social criticism contains, like the socialistic, many valuable elements which often leave Christians ashamed. In the Dutch liberalism of earlier liberal Christendom and in humanistic atheism, socialism is certainly not always in the forefront. The new world-religion of neo-Marxism, with all its schismatic sects and variants, may be on the advance and may to a great extent conquer the world (particularly the "intellectuals" and the "half-intellectuals"), but there is still much contravention. The old humanistic types of faith are re-emerging, just as Christendom grows weaker and more defenceless against the new world-religion of Marxism.

In trying to answer the question, "Whence social criticism?" we must look for the *feeding ground* of present social criticism on a deeper level than the evidence found on television and in the papers. The question concerns all the concrete needs and misery that make us sad, resentful, rebellious, or perhaps apathetic and resigned. The gulf between factual conditions and human ideals is too wide. This can be called the outward cause of social criticism. But *how* we criticize, and what the real *contents* of our criticism is, depends on our *view of life*. Whether this view of life is comprehensive or primitive does not matter; everyone in fact reacts spontaneously from his view of life in a *critical* or apathetic way.

Some observers have created a superficial view of man by saying that our present social criticism originates directly from "information" and from the scientific elaboration of information. This position is completely unacceptable. The evidence of so much violently opposing criticism about the same issues must surely put us on guard against making such a blunt error. Indeed, a view of man and a practical view of life both embodied in our personal and communal life are *the feeding-ground for a more outspoken criticism*.

In criticism (as the Greek origin of the word suggests), a sifting and separating process takes place, *whereby norms or criteria are implicitly handled*. When we consider thoroughly this criticism, we meet with ideals, values or norms which are considered to be generally valid. As these are not only valid for ourselves, they are therefore supra-individual and supra-arbitrary. On our present cultural level, the

125

different views of life have crystallised partially into a more explicit *theory in connection with human society*. This theory describes society's nature, structure, diversity, coherence, order and disorder, etc. In this respect, the different views of life that compete with one another are the embodiment of spiritual trends. The most developed views of society are those of orthodox Roman Catholicism, "Neo-Calvinism," Liberalism and that of Marxism, each with its own variants.

From this spiritual feeding-ground originates, in each case, a different criticism of society, because different norms (criteria, ideals and values) are applied. These differences are obscured by talking about "concrete models" as if they are neutral, hypothetic, and experimental thought-products, composed of "scientific data." This is not the case. The alternative models for another form of society conceal a load of ideology. In itself this concealment is not so bad, nor is it even avoidable. I merely find deplorable how man is seldom conscious that via a model he also propagates normative views of man and society. These are definitely not religiously neutral, but in their turn originate both historically and structurally from *faith*, religious experiences, religious representations and religious dogmas. Truly, a view of life and society is, according to its nature, stamped by a certain faith.

When we come across opposing models of changing structures of society we should, amongst other things, penetrate to the nature and origin of the social philosophical *structures of thought*.

These are the hidden players on the keyboard of the communication media. And we can discover them with the help of a consistent philosophical sociology.

The Meaning of Christian Philosophy

We are still left with one problem. Why are serious, socially interested and politically engaged Christians concerned with present social criticism? Genuinely believing, intelligent young people from Christian homes, even if they are critically inclined, seem to have no resistance to powerful, leftist social criticism. On this subject, orthodox ministers often express sharp and correct judgements, because they are trained to "test the spirits whether they are from God." What is so tragic about Protestantism is that it could not *grosso modo* develop a biblically founded scientific view of society.

Many complex causes are responsible for this problem, including the fact that all efforts in this direction have been tackled in a *theological* way. This approach has always been destined to failure because it is inadequate. We still have not severed links with the Medieval ground-scheme which suggests that whenever a certain thought system is Christian, then it is also theological, and if it is not theological, then it is not Christian but generally human, neutral, etc.

In the theological circle, the thought and ideal of intrinsically Christian thinking first came to the fore with A. Kuyper and H. Bavinck. Both of them, but especially Bavinck, realised that Christian scientific endeavour should begin with a Christian *philosophy*.

127

These ideas did not find much resonance in Reformed Protestantism, but neither were they contested. They were primarily forgotten and ignored, or were misunderstood and held under suspicion, particularly by theologians who subscribed to "conservative ideology."

We will not discuss this matter in detail, but I do think that as a result, Christianity has missed an opportunity to re-examine modern scientific thought. Christianity could have gotten a grip on the sciences of man and society that co-determine to such an important degree the diverse types of social criticism. In the *structure* of all special sciences, a philosophical view inevitably functions, however rudimentary or embryonic this may be. In a Christian social criticism, we dare not ignore science and may not suffice with the idea that redemption can only be obtained through the person and work of Christ.

The Need for a Christian View on Society

It is not adequate to show the way by annexing, as typically Christian principles, the generally human norms of righteousness, neighbourly love, liberty, humanitarianism, human equality, etc., which are acknowledged by practically all people. In fact, the blind can also sense that all ideologies write these values on their banners. Even the social-minded ministers and theologians during the French domination resoundingly proclaimed that liberty, equality, and fraternity were, indeed, central Christian virtues. Today, we hear similar proclamations about concepts

such as equality, democracy, anti-authoritarian structures of influence, social righteousness, peace, etc.,
which are not subsequently analysed in greater detail
in social theory. In other words, we have not built
up any social-scientific and political resistance to the
anti-Christian spirit of the age.

Meanwhile the spirit of the age uses these sciences
to direct the society in a leftist direction with arguments
and interpretations. The power of Marxist faith,
and especially the contents of this faith, embodied
themselves in a Marxist view of society and in a
Marxist scientific attitude. Christianity has nothing of
equal value to place over against this. Christianity *does*
have something of *more* value, namely the witness of
faith that the salvation of society was brought about
by the cross of Christ and will be realised through the
power of His resurrection. The fact that Christ points
the way to the creational order is only a rudimentary
belief among Christians, a relic of faith that has been
theologically and philosophically sterilised.

This gap cannot be filled by theological ethics,
a "theology of the world," political theology, social
theology, theology of art, theology of money and
whatever theologies are brought on the market. Not
even a theology of creational ordinances in Lutheran
terms, or a theology of natural rights in Roman
Catholic terms, can suggest an answer. The hope of
many Christians is fixed on these theologies, and on
what can be achieved internationally by "ecumenical
ethics" via the World Council of Churches. If
we distrust these options, which seems justified,

129

there appears to be no other way than resignation, verticalism, "front-shortening," or witnessing that "only one thing is necessary," etc. This latter point is essential but it is not the full truth, because the Truth is also the Life, and the Life is the fulness and perfection of the *liberated creation*.

In my opinion, Van Ruler has a point when he says that, to Reformed theology, the social gospel is not something alien; it saw the church rising from the kingdom and gives precedence to the kingdom. For this reason, we cannot think horizontally enough on the kingdom of God, and we can never take this present world seriously enough because the "coming age" is the redemption, the liberation, and the reorganisation of *this* dispensation.

Van Ruler is also right when he says that Reformed theology never recovered from the ambivalence of the doctrine of the two domains: "Since Calvin himself it has worked on a dualism of the spiritual and the natural." Whether Reformed theology will still get an opportunity for purification on this point remains a question for Van Ruler. "But it is worthwhile to work on this," he also says. However, it was not Van Ruler who made the breakthrough possible, for he was too much bound to this theological tradition, in which pre-Christian and pre-reformational views on reality are still virulent. Moreover, this is not only a theology but also a theological *tradition*.

In my opinion the fundamental breakthrough in re-organising *all* sciences (including theology) took place in the philosophy of the Cosmonomic Idea. The dotted lines implied in it for a Christian view of man and society designate the criteria by which a *Christian* criticism of society can penetrate from the religious centre into concrete political, economic, and other problems. The structural nature of all criticism of society requires that it be built as a pyramid standing on an apex. This apex is the starting point of a certain faith, whether that be Christian, half-Christian, or un-Christian faith. The ground motive or ethos manifests itself, controlled by this starting point. In its turn the ethos is the spiritual basis from which life and thought structures are formed.

Within the ethos, philosophical thought-patterns are decisive for the development of the fundamental concepts of the special sciences. The latter are thoroughly acquainted with the problems which confront us daily. In the 20th century, Christianity must not allow itself to pass over this issue and continue the futile efforts *linea recta*. Nor can we adopt theology "from out of the gospel" in order to take a critical look at life in the "worldly domain" and to have "normative concessions" in a "simple way." In practice, the "baptismal" dualism that coquets with the world only plays into the hands of the communist world-strategy.

The "verticalistic" faith of Christianity has no resistance because it has reduced and sterilised itself. In contrast, the humanistic belief in the self-redemption of (historical) man has, in fact, developed

131

diverse and serviceable thought models for social "structure-changes." In spite of its nihilistic and disintegrating phenomena, humanism still has the lead in our Western culture. The church, guided by theology, still follows in the steps of humanism, capitalism, socialism, communism, etc., in a hesitant or submissive way, as the spirit of the age demands. Our Saviour foresaw this when He asked: "However, when the Son of Man comes, will He find faith on the earth?" (Luke 18:8). All these contemporary adaptations to "the world" and its thought-structures only yield unintended losses to "the church."

CHAPTER 5

Groundlines for a Christian View of Society

WHAT IS ETHOS? What is the deepest motivation that drives and directs man and society? Our answer, in part, is the non-scientific or pre-scientific view of life. The summary term "view-of-life" encompasses a view of the origin, nature, and destination of man, of his different tasks, of community and of the most important relations in society, that is, of "society" as a whole.

A Few Important Characteristics of the View of Life

1. A view of life is neither of a theoretical nor a systematic nature. It reveals itself more or less consciously in fragmentary views, in spontaneous stands taken, and in our general attitude toward life. A *view* of life is part of the more encompassing *attitude* toward life that controls, more or less directly, not only practical knowledge and considerations but

133

also activities themselves.

2. It falls under conscious or unconscious *guidance* of what man believes in connection with those things of life about which science, as such, cannot give any explanation (origin and destination, cf. 1).

3. The Christian view of life reveals the need and the will to be guided by the Word of God. It admits to being very defective in its function. It gladly submits itself to be corrected by the Word and Spirit of God and does not allow itself to be *overruled* by scientific theoretical thought, but avails itself of the services of such thought. It has more confidence in a science that *intrinsically* sets itself the task to be *Christian* than in a science that revolves around the radical dogma of the (religious) apostate European culture. This culture follows the dogma of the fundamental autonomy and independence of the supposedly "pure" scientific thought. The latter is totally different from "believing in some or other incontrollable authority."

View of Society and View of Man

In a view of life, the view of man and of society are naturally closely interwoven and can hardly be kept apart. In the *Christian* view of life, the Christian faith plays an obvious and conscious role. In subordination to the revealed Word of God, we confess that man is created in the image of God and that human life and society stand under the law of God. We confess the law and will of God not only as a heteronomous arbitrariness of a "higher power," but as the blessed law of life which makes *true* life and society possible. Therefore, in Christ we see the fulfilment of the law and the new root from which Christian society can grow.

The Antithesis

Christianity and Humanism are not partial allies or reciprocally complementary partners; they are truly opposites. The religious "anti-thesis" is the life liquid that saturates the whole plant. Only the *degeneration* of the doctrine of common grace denies the radical character of the antithesis, of its thorough influence in concrete life, and discards it as an "overruled theological conception." In the long run, collaboration with a political party or labour union starting with this conviction would be detrimental. Even the church community is damaged and brought in serious danger by such collaboration. For this antithesis does not concern a "rational view," i.e., a human conception or rational antithesis, but the reality of the conflicting contradiction itself, as God promised and imposed it in the original promise of the Messiah of Genesis 3:15. This antithesis is revealed right through the Bible, up to the last pages, as a deep reality only visible to the vision of faith and practically experienced only in faith.

Every vision of society that denies the reality of

this antithesis concerns only an abstracted mental image of society. Such a vision damages and sterilises our faith life. Conversely, a vision of man's inner life of faith and his life in society, without any recognition of the antithesis, damages and de-Christianises concrete daily life. A view of society that considers it possible to isolate itself from the spiritual depth-dimension of human society is not successful at all.

The Gospel and our View of Society

We are confronted with the disheartening fact that Christianity in Holland is hopelessly divided on the question of the idea of society; each true Christian appeals to "the gospel" for his own view. This is the case in all political and societal groupings. At its best Christianity embodies a doubtful naïveness when it tries to organise and unite Christians on the basis of "the gospel" in every sphere of life, e.g., politics, science, trade, church, art or sport. One can honour and respect this wish and the broadmindedness it reflects, but it is misguided. Political actions directed toward this purpose are now characterised by well-meant but naïve short-sightedness, which proves its own impotence quite obviously. In the 20th century, man cannot ignore how Christianity, in spite of its intention to found itself on the gospel, has no agreement regarding the view of society.

No Common Christian Faith

One can claim that the norms and values of justice, peace ("harmony model"), neighbourly love, fellowship, etc., are typical Christian norms and values but that would be an error. Every one of these words refers to the will of God that is valid for all people (Ecc. 12:13). In fragmentary and extremely diverse ways these "norms and values" are more or less respected by different peoples in all times.

There is always a reason for social priorities propagated by people. These are always moments or elements from God's creational order. The contradictory (mis-)interpretations and realisations are due to the fact that humanity has severed these (generally recognised) norms from their divine Origin. We do not recognise Christ's central word of sanctification as the only way to an understanding of and real obedience to these norms (cf. Catechism of Heidelberg, answer 91).

Owing to the universal apostasy of mankind, there is no common faith with respect to God's will and law for society any more. This problem can be attributed to a deterioration of our belief in creation – a belief that is removed from the heart of the gospel (theologically and practically). Thus, the way is paved for a Greek philosophical view of reality concentrated in the idea of substance.

Reconsideration is Essential

In the 20th century we cannot pretend that our faith, without the intervention of tradition, of the church and of theological developments, is a direct, pure, and indisputable expression of what God's Word reveals to us. It is essential to distinguish the proper character of faith from the theological and ecclesiastical doctrines and from traditional interpretations – although these elements and the mutual relations cannot be ignored. Different philosophical and scientific theories and practical circumstances (e.g., socio-economical and ecclesiastical situations, the influence of leading personalities, etc.) had an influence on these intermediary instances, and they in their turn also *influence the contents of our faith.*

In my opinion (and I am no policy-maker), it is not advisable at this stage to be unduly anxious about the organisational power-formation in any sphere of life. This holds even in the political sphere, where power-formation ("influence" on policy of a government) should be an important goal. Against all pragmatic wishes of public opinion, and against the wish of the policy-making bodies of Christian organisations, we will have to go back to a *"reconsideration"* of the philosophical ("levensbeschouwelijke") principles that lead us. These principles have shown us the direction in the various social tasks and in the often difficult and intricate questions with which we are confronted.

Therefore, we should not dismiss the expression "from the gospel" as a meaningless banner; we must first try to come to a biblically founded view of "society," with guiding lines and indicators in practical life.

The Starting Point of a Christian View of Society

The Christian view of life has three sources of inspiration: the biblical faith of completed creation, radical corruption of all creatures because of apostasy, and the equally radical and total redemption and recreation through the work of Christ. We do not understand these sources *theoretically*, i.e., in a *theological* sense. Theology, according to its nature and task, offers a reflection on this "key of knowledge" exegetically, systematically, dogmatically, and dogma-historically. But the confession of *faith* mentioned above has a *different* nature and is of primary significance not only to theology but also to the view of man and society.

A fundamental error is committed when man identifies faith with theological theory. Even *faith* is not infallible; it is subject to deepening, enlightenment, strengthening, but not to discussion. For faith is the human *resonance* on the divine revelation-Word through God's Spirit. Only the theological reflection on this can be discussed. How this dialogue takes its course will depend on the influence of God's Word on the faith and thought of the discussion partners and on their theological training and intellectual capacity. These latter concerns do not relate to someone being a Christian in a central sense; the influence of God's Word, however, certainly bears on this point.

So this is our starting point – the pre-theoretical philosophical ("levensbeschouwelijke") choice of faith, which can now manifest itself in a view of life and in the view of society enfolded in it.

A Christian View of Society

From the above-mentioned starting point, we direct our attention to the insurveyable variety in creation, including human life. From our faith in creation, we *know* that God created all things "well" and "after their kind." The heavy accentuation of the Bible on creation "after their kind" is important. This idea is mentioned at least ten times in Genesis 1. In the light of this emphasis, we understand something about all the varieties we encounter in creation and in human life and society. As far as they enforce and reveal themselves in our experience as that which cannot be eliminated and cannot be ignored without punishment, they originate in God the creator's will. God reveals Himself in all these things.[27]

Sphere-Sovereignty

In the non-scientific view of life, the Christian faith in creation was the inspiration for the principle of

27. From a theological point of view, I want to note that the traditional differentiation between universal and particular revelation is not valid and must be completely eradicated. Some thinkers have accused theological horizontalism of stressing universal revelation at the cost of particular revelation. Or they suggest that the latter is absorbed by the former. These efforts, as forms of horizontalism themselves, remain entangled in the nature-grace-dualism, in which verticalism and horizontalism take turns in denying each other primacy. We should like to defend the thesis that there is only *one* reality, which is created in Christ.

"sphere sovereignty." We are not interested here in the historical question about whether Groen van Prinsterer or Kuyper coined this expression. Nor are we concerned about the philosophical question of whether the expression was well understood and treated in the past. There is much to say and to criticize about these issues, as the dissertation of J. D. Dengerink reveals.

Nevertheless, no matter how poorly this view may have been formulated, it still played a very important role in the Christian view of society. This view depended on the idea of sphere-sovereignty in its effort to Christianise organisations and practical action.

The "Free University" ascribes its name to this idea, although it has now renounced this relation and interprets the word "free" in a humanistic sense. The "Anti-Revolutionary Party" owes the fundamental articles of its programme of principles to it, although several of its leading figures rejected these principles as an "empty box," and the direction of this party was split in opposite directions. Up to 1946 the Reformed Churches ascribed to this same principle as its policy in connection with many social problems. However, when modern (existential) theologians took to the idea of "open-mindedness" – in those years still focussed on the moderate figure of Barth, they rejected, with the Reformed Churches, the theological doctrine of creational ordinances and silently sterilised article 2 of the Dutch Confession. These churches started losing their Calvinistic identity at a quickened pace

141

and are now left with those who wish to maintain themselves in a balance between "one-sided" views, afraid of everything that smacks of "polarisation."

Sphere-Sovereignty and Creational Belief

These references to the Free University, the Anti-Revolutionary Party and the Reformed Churches were a brief illustration of what happens when the *belief in creation* is no longer a living and life-giving *faith*. When such belief degenerates into "nothing but rational knowledge" it is not the "saving power of God."

Then one does not experience the "vision" on society given by this faith. One can start *practically* nothing with it. The way "von der Bibel zur Welt" is narrowed and its direction is altered to an "evangelical commandment of love." But this commandment is severed from the law of God in the creational order, so it is nothing but a sterile "inspiration" liable to many interpretations.

The "metaphysical" love of God in the redemption of Christ now becomes dialectically detached from or opposite to a sterile creational faith. Man can then indulge in endless theological discussions on the exegesis of Genesis 1 without being able to contribute anything to the revival of the creational belief. And this belief, as such, is not a result of the theological exegesis of the account of creation. Belief depends on the capitulation of man to God's *creational will*, revealed in God's *creational law*, which becomes (for faith in any case) visible in the creational word of God.

The preaching of reconciliation loses its basis and fruitfulness for practical life because we fail to understand that the cross of Christ was erected *in* and *out* of creation. In this way Christ could renovate the creation and maintain, redeem, and liberate from what is against its nature and bring it to fulfilment and completion. Such a mistaken belief in reconciliation, severed from a belief in creation, is a theological abstraction.

In this way theology, instead of indicating a direction, was shunted to a side track. Otherwise it would have maintained the full belief in creation and might have found a better formulation for the above-mentioned central principle for society. Perhaps "distinct responsibility," ("eigensoortige verantwoordelijkheid") or "individual independence" in the different spheres of life, could become a new expression for the direction that the Christian creational belief shows for the "society."

Alternative Societal Principles

From ancient times mankind, in so far as it revealed a certain level of cultural development, battled with the central problem of the limits of competency in the different forms of community, society and institution. The most deeply rooted form is the totalitarian view which considers society as one structural "whole," of which churches, states, families, businesses, etc., are "parts." This thought can never be reconciled with the biblical view, which sees a genuine totalitarian *spiritual* community embracing the whole of human existence in Adam or "the second Adam," and in whom, as in one "body," each "member" has its meaningful place and task (Rom. 12, 1 Cor. 12).

If man has appropriated a fundamentally totalitarian view on society, all that is left within this unbiblical cadre of a whole-parts scheme is to argue about the nature of the "autonomy" that the parts have in connection with the whole. From this scheme originates the fundamental principle of the Roman Catholic doctrine of society (in so far as it hasn't been neutralised by modernistic thought), namely the so-called "subsidiary-principle" in its somewhat divergent dual effect.

The original *"Reformational-Socialistic"* central principle for the definition of the competency-spheres of society and state was the principle of "functional decentralisation." The liberal principle at first seems to be the Christian fundamental principle of society, namely rejection of the intervention of the state and the separate authority of life sectors. There is a great deal of arbitrariness in the way man renounces this specific principle in the *liberal* circle (Christian education, the broadcasting law, the culture policy, etc.). Yet the liberal "do-it-yourself-mentality" is even more saturated with fundamental individualism than with a deepened Christian insight into the normative enkaptic structures of the different communities.

All these different *fundamental directions* in the *view of society* battle with the same problem. How do we

144

explain the mutual relation, coherence, and deeper unity of all the many different forms in which each, "according to its nature" guides and directs human life and community?

From this principle emerges the criterion for what is truly reaction or progression.[28] Seen in broad outline, only the Christian view of society points in the direction of the unfolding of life in all sectors "to their nature." Meanwhile, all the other fundamental principles (naturally in different tempo and intensity) suffocate life, build a wall around it, and begin to build a totalitarian and primitive structure. In support of this, practical political life follows diverse ideologies concerning humanity, equality of people, democratising, etc. Christians with little knowledge of the Bible and no Christian social-philosophical education have hardly any resistance to these temptations.

Society-View and Science

In the Christian view of life there should be no reason to raise suspicion about, or even to disqualify, scientific thought. The same criteria hold true for theology. Some theologians view the philosophy of the Cosmonomic Idea as a dangerous rival, but this is merely misunderstanding.

---

28. Cf. the scientific jubileum-oration of Prof. Dooyeweerd in "De Koninklijke Nederlandse Akademie van Weten-schappen," at its 150th anniversary in 1958, under the title: *Norms for discerning progressive and reactionary movements in the historic development.*

In our present culture there is hardly any significant social, political, or economical problem that does not require scientific assistance in order to be solved. Almost all political parties have scientific advice bureaux, major businesses have research departments, and churches have theologically instructed "leaders." Similarly, Christian activity, which determines its own position and resolutions in all spheres of life, can hardly manage without direct or indirect support from those who are trained in theoretical thought. We are merely acting in a *reactionary* manner when we sometimes assume that the good scientific direction and vision, which is necessary for correcting our modern societal problems, is found "directly out of Scripture" or directly out of "Scripture and confession." This assumption is not borne out in the sciences, nor in practice.

Scientific thought has its "specific nature;" it has a "structure" which gives it its identity and differs from the structure of non-scientific thought and experience. In each science, philosophy plays a concealed role in its *basis* and in the *background*. The moulding of concepts and thought patterns in science is directed and driven from its basis (the "transcendental ideas"). For this reason, it is essential that a Christian philosophy be developed. This study can show us the *internal* structural ways revealed in the nature of theoretical thought by the creational order. A Christian philosophy can also give direction, guidance, and support to scientific thought in the special sciences.

Philosophy and the Practical View on Society

The non-scientific view on society, politics, science, trade, sports, art, etc., can also receive important assistance from Christian philosophy. I am thinking specifically of a philosophical analysis of the modal aspects of reality, and also of a *philosophical* theory of the different *types* of society-structures and their enkaptic relations in society. These are profound and all-encompassing theories. They have been the basis of a constant dialogue between the leading thinkers of our Western culture throughout all centuries. Sometimes these theories are stated in an abbreviated and popularised form, as in the case of diverse "introductions" (the most recent is that of L. Kalsbeek). These introductions are a support for all those who in practice take up a leading position in a particular sphere of life.

The Urgent Need for Christian Special Sciences

Naturally, however, these introductions are not enough. In our times the different special sciences that examine different sectors and aspects of social life play a very important role. We find ourselves in a distressful position: we cannot do without this help, yet we are misled by it, because the development of Christian science is still in a preliminary stage. In a rather embryonic way, Christian science is presented by individuals and small study-groups – especially but not exclusively – organised by the "Vereniging voor

147

Calvinistische Wijsbegeerte."

In recent years, the Free University officially abandoned the ideal of searching for and developing a Christian science. In its annals can be seen several serious efforts – undertaken especially by theologians but also by other scholars – to formulate the "Christian principles for the different sciences."[29] Looking back now, it is astonishing in the light of Dooyeweerd's "transcendental criticism" that these efforts *had* to fail due to the inner structural law of theoretical thought itself.

I will not treat this problem here in detail. It is a very intricate philosophical matter and a delicate question. Theologians use this issue as a prestige-matter for theology, which should (according to Aristotle) be the "queen of the sciences" and ought to give guidance to the whole of life via the church. Theologians do not speak and think like this anymore, but this attitude nevertheless still *lives* in them and in the churches.

Ironically, theology (and especially theological ethics) acts *according to its nature* when it offers an opinion on social, medical, political, artistic, or other problems; theology *necessarily* follows in the footsteps of the "information" of the special sciences. The hidden, religious, philosophical powers act according to their nature and function intrinsically in the very

---

29. Cf. Dooyeweerd: *The Ecumenical-Reformational ground-motive of the Philosophy of the Cosmonomic Idea and the Basis of the Free University*, Farewell-lecture, 1965, in *Philosophia Reformata*, 1966.

fibre of the special sciences. These powers steer our thought in the direction of the ethos, following the spirit of the times. This takes place under the guise of the independence of "pure" science based on "pure facts."

Elaboration of a View of Society

The practical view of life, led by a belief, cannot (according to its nature) specialise and systematise. It cannot *apply* "faith," as if faith is a logically formulated recipe that functions as a major premise in a syllogism. This view of life cannot deduce societal, political, scientific, or artistic principles from the Bible in a logical deductive way, as rationalistic biblicism (in an old-fashioned or modern way) tries to do. The Christian view of life and society is a *witness*. It acknowledges and confesses that God created life, continuously maintains it, and guides it with His divine creator's will, which is revealed to us as the *creational order* and *creational law*.

This view doesn't imply any easy recipe for the solution of all problems. But it is part of the Christian attitude of life, which seeks the will of God in everything. It follows that man, in his theoretical-systematical thought, follows the dotted lines and chalk stripes that God put down as a trail in his creational order.

The laws for scientific thought – now diligently investigated by methodology, hermeneutics, and the theory of science – themselves judge the mutually combating theoretical systems, models and

149

hypotheses. They assist or restrain man in the way he wants to act in an "a priori" fashion. We are not led by "unprejudiced" science; we lead the sciences from out of our deepest convictions, our religious attitude toward life. In our heart lies the starting point of our life-course.

In the creational order this way was made. Only when the Spirit of God takes us by the hand are we not led astray by the spiritual powers that conceal themselves in philosophy and science. We are defended against those powers that claim with mighty pretentions the guidance of life and the guidance of theoretical thought and knowledge.

Christian Social Sciences

For the exceedingly complicated, modern, social problems we need the support of the social sciences. These sciences must be practised in such a way that they do not *exalt* themselves above us, the non-specialists, but, centred in the same belief, will trace with us the structures of all God's works "under the sun." This is our commissioned task. Science should adopt other means than acting as the policy-maker in practical life. These two realms cannot ignore each other. At the moment, we as theoretical and practical people lead each other from "the frying-pan into the fire." In this state of spiritual emergency, it is important for Christian scholars to develop and apply a Christian-philosophical critique of science, especially in the territory of the "social sciences."

By applying such a critique, we will learn to

150

give scientific answers when sociologists state that authority is the same as accepted power, or when churches pretend to pronounce with authority on every social problem. By doing this we will learn "to speak with the enemy at the gate," as long as the enemy does not ignore us or avoid us.

CHAPTER 6

The Social Meaning of the Gospel

A Biblical Basis for Christian Living in the Secular World

IN BOTH THE Old and New Testaments we find a number of social prescriptions for the Israelites and the Christians in the first century after Christ. All these commandments and statutes stem from the central commandment in which love for God and for our fellow men are connected.

In the past, very little attention has been paid to the comment of Christ that everything, not merely the whole law but also the prophets, hangs on this two-sided commandment of love. In the language of the Bible, "prophets" describes not only what we now call the great prophets and the twelve minor prophets, but also the writers of the historical books, such as Moses, Joshua, and the author of I & II Kings, etc. Even the Psalms and Proverbs are regarded as prophetic books. The expression "law and prophets" describes the whole Old Testament, including the

153

account of God's work in creation.

We know from the Scriptures, and in the light of the Scriptures from our experience in daily life as well, that God has revealed His will in all the works of His hands. When we say this we are speaking, for example, of laws of nature, natural moral laws, ordinances, and institutions of human society such as the state, marriage, church, etc. In the central commandment of love all these ordinances are united and brought into focus. They are not focussed in a logical unity, but in the divine unity of the central twofold commandment of love.

However, in His revelation of the law, God did not restrict the meaning of this central focus of love to the specific commandment He gave in the Scriptures. The poet in Psalm 119:96 says: "thy commandment has no limit." As he wrote this Psalm the poet was probably in prison. All day and night he was studying the law (which probably included the history of his people, the "prophets"). Nobody knows how many days or weeks or, possibly, years he was doing this. Nevertheless, many times he prayed: "Teach me" (Psalm 119:33 etc.).

The will of God was not given in a clear-cut way for every concrete situation. There was no absolute prescription that was valid at all times and in every situation. Paul wrote to the Philippians (Philippians 1:9–10), urging "that your love may grow ever richer and richer in knowledge and insight of every kind and may thus bring you the gift of true discrimination."

The Lord did not give His people absolute and detailed commandments and prohibitions for every possible case, question, or situation. Even in the days of Moses, the book of the law was not complete and did not regulate everything. The last chapter of Numbers, for example, shows that the law on inheritances needed further amplification. A phenomenon such as polygamy was obviously taken for granted (Deut. 21:15–17). The law of God was still growing and even changing in different times and circumstances. Even in the letters of Paul we find quite a different approach to various concrete problems compared to that taken in the Old Testament, although the main features are the same.

But what of today? In general, one question is central. What are the concrete regulations by which Christians must live after the days of the apostles? This has been a question for Christians through all ages and in all cultures up to the present day.

In the period between the Old and New Testaments, the Jews had already tried to resolve this vital question. The law of the Old Testament does not always fit the real-life situation of succeeding ages. However, the Orthodox Jews wanted, at all cost, to keep every jot and every tittle of the law. In order to do this, they developed a broad and very detailed network of commandments and prohibitions, all of which were logically derived from passages in the laws of Moses.

But in this kind of Jewish theology the living

155

faith faded away. The scribes were trying to confine the living stream of the will of God in history to hundreds of separate prescriptions and prohibitions. These they regarded as valid in every circumstance. And they pronounced condemnation on the masses who did not know all these specific laws.

Very soon after the first age of Christianity, the church and the "church fathers," influenced by Jewish orthodox tradition and pagan Stoic ethics, adopted the same methods. Alongside Jewish casuistry, a Christian casuistry came into existence. Again, after the Reformation, the same development occurred in many Protestant circles. This tendency was probably more marked in the Calvinist tradition than in the Lutheran tradition. In the Lutheran tradition, antinomianism was stronger while in the Calvinist tradition legalism developed.

Today, throughout the entire Christian world, we are still struggling with the problems of what we commonly call "ethics." It is discussed in the form of social ethics, personal ethics, theological ethics, philosophical ethics, or whatever else we wish to call the issues in question. One central question is at issue: How do we know the will of God in our modern life, which involves problems that are not mentioned and could not be mentioned in Holy Writ?

We could approach this question in the following way. Must we go further in the line of casuistry, the line of the Jewish scribes, exploring the Scriptures with the purpose of deriving prohibitions and prescriptions from biblical statements or propositions? I am convinced that this would be an incorrect method to adopt. I shall try, therefore, to sketch the main features of an alternative which, in my opinion, is more biblical.

As I suggested above, the whole will of God is revealed in just one command, in one word, and in the deepest sense, in one Person. God is love and He has revealed Himself in Jesus Christ, who is love. In Him and through Him the will of God appeared as love, formulated in the central commandment of love, and fulfilled in the person and work of Christ.

Every other formulation or concrete expression of the will of God depends on this central commandment. But what does it mean to say "depends on"? We may use the idea of the refraction of one ray of white light into all the colours of the rainbow as it passes through a prism. As refracted light, we can see all these colours separately, but in fact they "depend on" the white light of the one ray. So all the commandments, prohibitions, statutes, ordinances of God display an inner coherence and a central unity in the one commandment of love, which is fulfilled and realised in Jesus Christ.

The will of God was revealed in the way God created all things, giving each creature its own character, its own nature, its own law of life. And all these laws of life, all these creational ordinances, are bound together in the creational order concentrated in the one will of God: the service of love in God's kingdom, which embraces the whole creation, including human society.

In every situation of our daily life we are always looking for the right decisions and the right acts. Intuitively, consciously, or unconsciously, we are looking for the norms and the normative factors to determine and direct our acts and purposes. In contemporary life, as we seek answers to the day-to-day issues of life, we are always influenced, directly or indirectly, by the theories and conclusions of the various sciences: theology, philosophy, social sciences, economics, political science, jurisprudence, aesthetics, linguistics, history, etc. Whether consciously or unconsciously we do use the results of science. All these sciences deal in a basic way with the laws of life in the various aspects of the creational order.

This role that science plays in modern life has given modern Western culture great expectations of science. As a result, the importance of science is over-estimated at the expense of the more important influence of ideological powers in human society.

At present it is becoming clearer that the ideological powers of this world submit all the sciences to their own non-scientific purposes in a radical way. This submission is evident in materialistic and/or political ideals and idols. In the Bible we are warned against the spiritual powers of the air (Ephesians 6). These are indeed the guides of human society, which fight against the spirit of Christ.

But what is the reaction of God's people in the

modern world to these powers of secularisation? I believe there are two main types of reactions. (At this point I must interrupt my main argument with a somewhat lengthy digression.) The first type of reaction by Christians to the modern powers of secularisation is negative, and the second is more positive. However, in my opinion, both need to be corrected by biblical insights.

The negative reaction of many Christians to the secularisation of human society is reactionary in the historical sense. Being afraid of secularisation, and rightly and earnestly convinced that we always need to go back to the Bible, these Christians try to find the way of obedience for modern life in the old Jewish and Roman Catholic fashion. From the Holy Scriptures they try to collect those passages that appear to be relevant. Then they try to apply them to the questions that arise in our complex and differentiated society.

These Christians are inclined to neglect the sciences, or at least such "humanities" as psychology, sociology, economics, and political theory. They do not trust these sciences and, to a certain extent, they are right in not doing so. But their method is wrong. By reverting to the prescriptions of Jewish ethics, they are really adopting a reactionary attitude. Although they may be acting out of a sincere concern for a biblical life, they fail to realise that God has revealed His will not only in the Bible but in the whole creational order. The Bible has a central and most important place in the whole revelation of God, but it should not be divorced from the totality of the creation in which God has revealed Himself.

There is a sound element in this reactionary attitude – the authentic biblical acknowledgement that in the first place we need the guidance of the Holy Spirit. The fear of the Lord is the beginning of knowledge. So it is quite correct that the main accent should be placed on the Scriptures. But it is quite wrong to go back to the method of the Jewish scribes in using the Scriptures to answer questions about ethics and human conduct.

The second type of reaction by some Christians to the powers of secularisation uses the same principal method as the first. They differ from those who hold the more reactionary attitude in being more positive in their acknowledgement and evaluation of the guidance of modern life by the sciences. Except where a scientifically based solution of modern problems literally contradicts a clear statement in the Bible, many Christians and theologians are inclined to follow the trends of modern society in politics, science, arts, education, law, morals, and customs. They see no other alternative to being conservative in a theological sense. They want to adopt a position more or less half-way between conservative theological ethics and the position of modern society. They are afraid of what they call "polarisation."

Now, my very short excursion into the main types of Christian positions in response to secularisation in modern society may be too simple. But it may also be sufficient for our critical look at the biblical alternative to traditional ways of applying the Bible to modern social problems.

Resuming my argument, I return to the biblical message of creation. God created everything by calling it into existence according to its own kind (Genesis 1). According to Ecclesiastes, it is the task of man "to seek and to search out by wisdom all that is done under heaven." In the Bible we cannot find those things that God has revealed in other words or in the works of His hands. So in society we need to be wise, to be full of love, and also to serve the Lord with "all your mind," as Jesus said.

"With all our mind" – what does this mean in modern Western culture? Here the role of science in social life must be mentioned. Science should not have the guiding role, but it does have a very important role. The sciences themselves are always guided by one spirit or another. In their inner structure the sciences show a dependence on non-scientific attitudes, basic motives or driving forces. These can be analysed and systematised by philosophy.

Guided by the biblical message of creation and the social meaning of the gospel, we are called to deal with sociology and social philosophy. However, as we noted in chapter 5, the hidden religious-philosophical powers, function in the very fibre of the social sciences. They steer our thought in the direction of the spirit of the age. This occurs under cover of the dogma of "pure," independent, empirical science, which is supposed to be dealing with "pure facts." In the "social sciences" we find that the forming of concepts, defining of problems, and the resultant "information" is often coloured by ideology.

There is now a particular need for Christian social sciences. Fortunately, we have some helpful foundational material for this task in the pioneering work already done by men like H. Dooyeweerd and D. H. T. Vollenhoven, and by others who have followed in their steps. Their foundational work has given us a theoretical framework. Now we can try to follow the path that God has put in His creational order as a trail for us.

In God's creational order, and in His continual activity in maintaining that order, the way of life is set out. We can follow this way only with the guidance of God's Spirit. The spirits of this present age have concealed themselves in a supposedly neutral science, and their power is tremendous. But in the light of the Scriptures we can unmask this deceptive power.

It is not so easy to be a devoted Christian if one is a politician, trade union official, scientist or artist. We still lack a political confession of faith, and a Christian view of society, ideal of science, and inspiration for artistic activity. In the Christian political parties of Europe there is still a semblance of a theoretical programme based on principles. But at present there is little common faith confessed in those programmes.

This problem cannot be attributed solely to the inevitable contemporary character of these political principles and their formulation. Neither is it merely due to the complexity of present-day problems. In part, at least, this lack of common faith is due to the weakness of our belief. In the confusing diversity of modern life, we have not sought a way of life adapted to the creational order. We have adopted the idea of non-Christian social sciences, which bear every conceivable hue of humanistic thought.

In the previous paragraph I suggested that something is lacking. What would the situation be like if we had the common faith that is lacking at present? Would the situation then be any easier for Christians? The answer must be: No!

We *would*, however, be fighting the good fight, and no more is asked of us by God. We would still be ridiculous and powerless in so far as this world is concerned, but we would have a clear conscience and the knowledge that the crown of victory is awaiting us in the life hereafter. More than this has never been promised to us. Being salt and being light in the world does not imply that believers will obtain power or positions of influence in society. They will show to all who struggle with social problems the road map of God's creational order, which indicates the main roads as well as the side tracks.

From this map we also see how God's roads, set out in this creation, run via Calvary to the equally catastrophic and redemptive final judgement. It is this road map of the Kingdom of God that indicates for all creatures and sectors of social life their own laws of life and domain.

Therefore, the central "principle" of a Christian view of society is that of the particular or specific responsibility of each sector of society. Or, stated differently, there are in human society various domains of freedom under the law of God, each with its own specific character.

Man can never exhaust the full content of faith, as it relates to the creational order, by employing one or two deficient formulations. What is most important is that in every sector of human life we seek the will of Him who maintains and effectively validates His creational order in judgement and grace. In this search there is the promise of "finding." But the revelation of God always remains concealed from autonomous thought.

Should we choose to be liberal or socialistic? It is difficult to avoid being drawn in by the powerful ideas stemming from this well-known dilemma of modern life. In this dilemma, old and very powerful forces of a religious origin, operating through philosophy and the sciences, lay claim on the thought patterns forced on us through our culture. It is no use trying to solve this dilemma by looking for a precarious and untrustworthy balance in some golden mean between these two poles.

What we need is a clear perspective on the totalitarian idolatries to which both the above trends are committed. Neither of them has any place for a heartfelt faith in the saving grace of God alone. This saving grace operates in and through the creational law, calling into being all the various spheres of life, each with its own distinctive character for mutual help and support. Instead of this faith, people bow to the Baal of ever-increasing prosperity and the Astarte of distributing material prosperity. Both operate from a common jealousy and greed, which often pose as "humane" concerns.

Now we can recognise the religious depth dimension in the sociopolitical trends of modern Western society. So we may ask: in what ways can God's common grace, through such trends, influence humanity "for good"? This "good" from the side of God is brimful of forbearance, the postponement of judgement and a gracious calling to the world so it may still direct itself to its Creator and Redeemer.

In most countries we, as Christians, should use every possibility to counter the power of humanistic forces with our own organisational power. However, any Christian organisation is doomed if it does not primarily seek its power in the spiritual power of its witness: all earthly welfare – if it really is welfare – must be accepted at the cross of Christ with the hands of faith. Everything else is merely curing the symptoms. Such tasks are important, nevertheless, and with these we may indeed fill our lives as long as God gives us time and opportunity, "so long as it is day." But we should not cause the Christian witness to be misunderstood, as if any real welfare in this world is "loosely available" apart from Calvary. Anyone who promotes such a misunderstanding is anti-social and has no love for his neighbour.

The central normative principle for society (the specific task of the different spheres of life) needs to be concretised and refined further with the aid of a Christian social philosophy. This philosophy must do justice, from its foundation in faith, to the many-sided normativity to which every form of human community-life is subject, according to the creational order. In the modern world, our thinking about society always involves some cooperation with social philosophy and social sciences. But it is here, in social philosophy and the social sciences, that Christian thought has as yet only taken a first step. It needs to develop further in order to keep pace with the differentiation and complexity of our modern Western culture.

CHAPTER 7

Church and Politics

The Problem and its Current Relevance

THE PROBLEM UNDER discussion has been a lively issue throughout the history of the church. As Christians, how can, and should, we live in this world? Today the problem is focused on the task of the officially organised church, with its different services. Observers wonder whether this church can and should play a role in relation to politics and to society in general.

Let us begin by looking at the current relevance of this question. Through the news media we are aware of the enormous world-wide political interest in the election of the Pope. We are aware of the international discussion and indignation concerning actions of the World Council of Churches in its battle against racism. We are also aware of the pastoral letters, episcopal declarations, and synodical decisions on such vital questions as abortion, developmental aid, euthanasia, homosexuality, extramarital sex, the neutron bomb, the problem of the Jews and the Arab world, the multi-nationals, nuclear energy, and politics in Southern Africa. How should we face these issues?

An Answer in Principle

The religious revival that took place in a section of the reformed community in the Netherlands offered, in principle, an answer to our question. The answer came in the advocation of the principle of "sovereignty in its own orbit (sphere)." In spite of all the personal interconnections between people in political parties, churches, schools and trade unions, those who advocate this principle want to distinguish consistently between the different official domains. They want to honour the mutual boundaries of competence and the different nature of societal structures with their typical laws.

Remaining Problems

One problem, however, remains unresolved in this principle, and this problem concerns the church. To what extent can ecclesiastical supervision, admonition and discipline take place without assailing the Christian freedom of church members? This is an internal problem for the church, but it also has external ramifications. When should the church as proclaimer of the Word of God officially address the government, commerce, trade unions, sport, the press, etc., and in relation to what questions?

In the past, these practical questions were not considered theoretically, but people still had a very good and practical solution. The intention of preaching was to emphasise from the pulpit the actual problems existing in society, but not to "deal with" those problems. The calling of the congregation to serve God in "all spheres of life" was pointed out, but the task of making this concrete in the practical issues of life was left to concerned Christian organisations and to the investigation of Christian associations. Christian institutions and weekly newspapers (although confusingly called "ecclesiastical associations" and "ecclesiastical press") were valued and commended from the pulpit as signs, principles, and configurations of the *kingdom* of God. They were *Christian* activities, non-ecclesiastical, but Christian.

This practical answer, according to the above-mentioned principle of "sovereignty in its own orbit," gave a certain clarity to pre-war Reformed life in the Netherlands for approximately half a century.

Crisis

During the thirties, disintegration was already beginning to take place. The unresolved problems opened the door through which the spirit of the age could easily enter the churches, in spite of an initially rigid maintenance of the ecclesiastical confessions. The humanistic spirit of the irrational "philosophy of life" and the spirit of historical relativism cleared a way for themselves and could not be stopped by either confession or orthodox theology. Neither the church nor Christian life could be safeguarded against the spiritual powers of the world merely by church orders, theologies, and philosophies. "This kind cannot come out by anything but prayer and fasting" (Mark 9:29).

At the same time Christian political thought also declined. It was hollowed out and adapted to modern thinking, guided by the same philosophical views which were concealed in the new modern theological schools. The former Kuyperian-Reformed world, born in the religious revival of the last century, collapsed in the fifties and sixties. It does not exist anymore.

The Failure of Ecumenical Efforts

The principle of sovereignty in its own orbit, which was based on the Christian belief in God's creation of everything after its kind, was replaced by the ecumenical approach. On close scrutiny the church's solutions to social and political questions, using this approach, do not impress.

It can be said of almost all the pronouncements of the church against nuclear armament, racism, militarism, and developmental aid, for example – that these are formulated so diplomatically that they always leave a back door open. In most cases they are only clear and unambiguous on the obvious questions where all Christians, and many non-Christians, already agree on the answers. There is no unity in testimony or service, either in typical ecclesiastical matters or in social and political questions.

A Critical Question

In this confusion in ecclesiastical and Christian practice, a critical question emerges. Would it not be better
for the church to restrict herself in official services
to her primary task and leave the social and political
problems for discussion and judgement to her members, operating individually or in private groups and
Christian organisations?

I believe that in principle this is still the correct
answer to the question we are discussing. This does
not imply that all the problems would be solved. Our
theme, however, is the place and task of the church
in connection with political and social questions. Let
us view this problem once more. The problem has a
practical side as well as a theoretical side.

The Practical Point of View

The practical problems are obvious. There was a time
when the minister was the advisor of the congregation on many questions. Just before the war we had
in the Netherlands a voluminous book with the title, "What Does the Minister Say About This?" This
book was presented by the publisher as a complete
Christian ethic for all life's problems.

This tradition is significant and still alive,
although not as strongly. The official word of
synods, theologians and ministers has lost a lot of its
authority. But at the same time the idea of the church's
competence to pronounce on various questions has
been greatly encouraged by theology. For this reason

171

we are continually confronted, especially in practical life, by questions of competence and the boundaries of ecclesiastical competence in particular.

What are the church and its office bearers permitted to say and do when judging controversial practices in politics, in private life, in society? Are the office bearers of the church allowed to judge everything because their calling is to radiate the light of God's Word? Do they have the right and is it their duty to pronounce judgement on various practical questions from the pulpit? Should they do this with the authority of their office binding the consciences of believers in the name of God? And what happens if one office bearer agrees and another disagrees?

We could also put the question in another way. Do we expect too much from the Bible? Fifteen years ago there was a "singing minister" who had a song on one of his LPs with a recurring line about how the Bible gives the answer to all the questions in our life. Somebody retorted: "Then it's a pity that our Bible editions don't have an alphabetical index."

A Practical Solution

To help our reflection on these practical questions, I would like to offer the following example. I think we should keep in mind the life and work of Paul. The apostle was very conscious of his religious calling to be a minister, and he had the audacity to prescribe and to forbid. But he did not degenerate into a busy-body, or an authoritarian, or a dictator. At the same time, he did not approve of indifference to permissiveness. There were times, however, when he chose not to force an issue, trusting that through God's Spirit the correct insight would dawn on people later, perhaps under the influence of his letters.

Paul also distinguished in I Corinthians 7 between what he said himself and what the Lord said. He did not consider his own opinion as unimportant, because he was conscious of possessing the Holy Spirit, and therefore he quite frankly offered his views. But he did not identify his opinion with the Word of God itself.

The church, however, still struggles with the problem of its leadership. In the course of the centuries this has led to several theological and philosophical theories.

Parallel Problems for the State and Political Thought

The problem concerning the extent and boundaries of the church's authority has a parallel in public life. Throughout history, there have been tremendous problems associated with the boundaries of state power and authority. Two extreme positions have been totalitarian omnipotence and individualistic chaos.

For a thousand years a struggle went on in Europe between the popes and the heads of the various states. In that struggle the *Roman Catholic theological doctrine* of the supremacy of the church in the name of God could not be maintained. So within society

173

as a whole, in the last century, the problem of state power was dealt with in the light of the "subsidiary principle." Simply stated, the higher can only interfere in the life of the lower if the higher finds it necessary to do so in its own interest.

Socialism developed the doctrine of functional decentralisation by which the central state authority grants a relative autonomy to non-political social committees. This principle also originates from the idea of the state as the last and highest authority, granting authority to others.

Here I should also refer to the *French Revolution*, which brought about a rigorous separation of church and state, each having omnipotence in its own orbit.

These three doctrines are examples of the moderation of the totalitarian power of the state in relation to the church and to other social structures and groups. I think it is important for politicians, and for us in our political thinking, to distinguish these doctrines, but it is even more important to detect the common fault in them.

The three principles (Roman Catholicism, socialism, and liberalism) are all based on a similar philosophical view: the community of the state is the whole, and the other societal relationships and communal institutions are *parts* of the whole. Wherever this scheme of the whole and its parts is put into practice, it offers no resistance at all to totalitarian omnipotence. On the contrary, it paves the way for such power.

According to the traditional semi-Christian scheme of two domains in human life – a natural one and a supernatural one – we see a tendency to totalitarian politics in the state and totalitarian politics in the church as well.

Sovereignty in Its Own Sphere

Inspired by the biblical teaching on creation, Abraham Kuyper developed in a practical way the principle of "sovereignty in its own sphere." He developed this idea from his experience in battling the liberalistic state absolutism of his time. This state absolutism occurred both in the democratic form of socialism and in the aristocratic form of liberalism.

Kuyper's development of this principle was not primarily philosophical in the scientific sense of that word. He was above all a practical politician and statesman as a member of parliament and later as prime minister. The deepest impulse for his thought and his practical struggle was the Christian belief that everything in human life, society, and in the various structures of communal relationships ought to develop according to its own creational nature or law of life. This belief gave depth and practical relevance to the Christian faith in creation that had not been attained before.

However, Kuyper was not always consistent in his development of this new insight. As a result, there were some unresolved questions in connection with the principle he adopted. Sometimes he confused sovereignty in its own sphere with the principle of the autonomy of the parts granted by the state as the whole.

Church and Politics/Christians and Politics

Following the demise of the principle of sovereignty in its own sphere and the consequent collapse of the Kuyperian-Reformed world, the relationship between church and politics has changed in the Netherlands. The ecumenical approach has suggested other models for Christians – e.g., the church exists for the world, or the church is the champion of the poor.

This leads us to consider some important questions. Is it right to say that Christians in the political field should fight for the interest of the church, for Christian schools, for Christian morals in public life? Up to a certain point I could say yes in response to this question, but it is a qualified yes! Christians are not called to promote all kinds of Christian interests by political means. Our first responsibility is to ask what the will of God is for the state according to its own nature. If we do this we will get quite a different answer to the question of the Christian's task in the political field.

The primary concern of the state as a public community is to do justice to all its citizens. It is the main and distinctive task of the state to provide justice for its citizens personally, and justice in relation to the communal relationships or societal forms of human life. More precisely, the state's task

176

is to provide public justice. It is not concerned with all the issues of internal private justice within the societal associations. Each societal association has to maintain justice in its own orbit – the church, the industrial enterprise, the societal structures. Between individuals, and between individuals and the societal structures, the state is to provide and to maintain righteous relations.

A member of the government, therefore, should not pursue his own interests, nor the interests of his special group, whether Christian or not, but the *public interest* of the whole state community; he should pursue *public righteousness*. Politicians may operate from different points of view as to what society and the state ought to do, and what they personally think is best for the whole state community. As representatives of different political parties, they will have different insights on these questions. But each politician or member of parliament should seek just order in public life.

The law should maintain and, where necessary, restore that just order and prevent disorder. For example, it would be righteous for the state to supply different kinds of non-government schools, Christian schools as well as humanistic schools, for those citizens who wish to educate their children according to their own convictions. As citizens, they, along with all others, pay taxes to the state to provide schools. Why should the state not supply separate non-government schools for Christians, humanists, or special ethnic groups?

Church and Politics

I have already distinguished *church* and politics on the one hand, and *Christians* and politics on the other. A group of Christians is not necessarily a church. Of course, in the New Testament the term "church" often appears to have different connotations. On many occasions it is used to refer to the body of Christ, the spiritual communion in the Holy Spirit, which expresses itself in worship but also in the Christian way of life in families, in master/servant relations, etc.

But the Christian family, for example, is not a little church in the sense of an organised community with office bearers. In our complex modern society, Christian colleges, schools, student associations, choral societies, or political parties are not typical churches but private activities and private associations of *Christians*.

This point is worth keeping in mind. Although the church leadership may have spiritual interests in common with all these kinds of Christian relationships, church authority is usually restricted to the boundaries of the task of the church in preaching the gospel, providing the sacraments, educating the youth in the main doctrines of the Bible and the church's confession, and in fulfilling the deacon's office. The church has no calling, no task to prescribe political choices, conjugal choices, or economic choices to her members.

The church must preach that the members in all spheres of their lives should seek the will of God; church leaders do not have the task of working out and prescribing what such revelation might mean in practice. This is not their task, even after careful preparation and discussion by study committees of theologians together with people of practical experience in the relevant areas of life. The church should not become involved at this level because it is not the task of the church. The office bearers of the church cannot possibly be acquainted with the many typical problems of modern life.

We also need to consider this issue in connection with the historical development and differentiation of human society.

Church and History

The church in New Testament times and the period immediately following cannot be compared to the churches of our modern pluralistic society. The historical process of differentiation, in which different kinds of societal structures developed their distinctive forms from the primitive clan-society, results from an historical cultural law. This process is universally recognised in the historical development of all cultures.

For this reason, the church in a modern society is no longer the all-encompassing communion of believers with an extended family relation. As soon as the church shows totalitarian tendencies, as happens both in the Roman Catholic church and some orthodox Protestant churches, she is reactionary in the historical sense of this term.

So the church, in relation to politics, must be careful to restrict her activities, including her sermons, to her own central and very important task of preaching the gospel of Jesus Christ. This is most important for politics, as well as other issues of human life. A faithful preaching of the gospel of Jesus Christ proclaims the Lordship of Jesus over all state governments and all the activities of citizens in every sphere of their lives.

But only the Word of God has the right to monopolise our life in a totalitarian way, since God is the only Lord of the whole of life. The preaching of the church should never attempt to usurp the place of God by pretending to have a totalitarian monopoly over our lives.

Christians and Political Parties

We are left with one unsolved problem. It is the task of political parties to unite common insights of citizens concerning the direction and policies for political action. Political parties must try to gain influence through the political power processes. It may be that in a particular population there are too few Christian citizens with common political insights to have any chance of gaining political power. Christians in this situation are faced with a question. Should they abandon the attempt to form a Christian political party?

In my opinion the answer depends on many factors in each particular situation. There is no universally valid formula.

One could conclude, as often happens, that a Christian political party, even though it has no chance of ever gaining the political power of government, should nevertheless be established as a public witness. We ought to seek the will of God in the political area of life as well. However, it might in some situations be more to the point to avoid this public witness. Christians could move in a different way, through pressure groups or personal contacts with politicians on specific issues of practical concern.

These two possible ways of proceeding could, in certain circumstances, be combined. As I have suggested, it depends on many cultural, spiritual, and political factors operating in each situation. For these reasons the central question of politics should be answered by Christians in their own geographical situation. But the issue does have to be considered by Christians as private citizens, among whom the ministers, Christian theologians and Christian philosophers should be very welcome to take their place – not as church office-bearers but *as private citizens*.

CHAPTER 8

Sovereignty in the Individual Sphere and the Unity of Life

WE OFTEN ENCOUNTER these two well-known expressions in the work of Abraham Kuyper and in the language of the "Reformed world" influenced by him. It seems to be difficult to find any connection between the two; they suggest quite opposite meanings. There seems to be a tension between the unity of life and the diversity of life.

The necessity of reflecting on this problem is evident. At present we are experiencing a previously unknown development in the different spheres of life. Politics, sports, medicine, economics, leisure, and the book market – all these and many other spheres make life completely insurveyable. In one area we might see an enormous development, of which people working in other areas have no idea. The attention of modern man is captivated by so many things that life appears to be a confusing multiplicity.

At the same time, however, people are trying

not to get lost in this chaos. A mainstay is sought in a simple all-encompassing viewpoint. This can be found in a political or an ecclesiastical ideal, in a predominating striving for pleasure, in sport, in science, in marriage or family life, etc. This mainstay is sought in something that stands central in the individual's own life. For a Christian, the central ideal is to live according to God's will in all things and to serve God and one's neighbour in love.

Let me now give an example of how the diversity of life and the unity of life are diametrically opposed. From my pastoral practice I remember a man who asked me to help him with preparatory arrangements for a divorce. One of his three children was ill. His wife deserted him after having repeatedly committed adultery, and she lived alone in a room somewhere in another city. Initially I helped him to find a housekeeper to look after the family. Shortly afterwards this man married his housekeeper. There was mutual affection and I solemnised this second marriage in church.

Everyone in this situation, however, was confronted with a problem. The man struggled with the problem of applying for a divorce, because God's commandment says: You shall not commit adultery. The woman's problem was the admonition of Jesus that whoever marries a divorced person also commits adultery. Together with members of the church council, I asked myself whether these facts were not an impediment to an ecclesiastical solemnising of this second marriage. How should the officials of the Civil Service and the judge act? If they were Christians, should they in every respect comply with the wishes of this man?

Several issues were at stake here. Do we have only one commandment in this case ("You shall not commit adultery") as a distinct guide for all these people, i.e., for the official, the judge, the minister, the housekeeper, and the man in question? Must every function and task be tested by the unity of only this commandment, or is there any tension between the unity of this commandment and the different callings and duties?

Let me offer a more recent example. A minister said he could not see his way to preach about the commandment on the observance of the Lord's Day the following Sunday after the congregational council had met on Monday to discuss the possibility of opening the swimming-bath on Sunday. One of his elders voted for opening it on Sundays. Should this elder have been admonished?

Christianity has always had to struggle with this kind of problem. One can even say that the heathen of the pre-Christian era were already faced with this issue. We can formulate this problem quite simply. A person wants to live according to one clear, predominating, and inspiring life-ideal but is often led astray in practice. One is forced by circumstances to act contrary to one's convictions, or one is compelled to compromise, or to accept a half-hearted solution

185

which satisfies nobody.

The pagan philosopher Cicero offered his solution to this problem: he said there are ordinary duties that hold good universally, and one dare not come into conflict with these duties. But there are high ideals that cannot be achieved by everyone – perfect duties that cannot be imposed on everyone.

Some further advice was offered by the first Christian moralist, Ambrose, who was bishop in Milan in the 4th century and played a major role in the conversion of St. Augustine.

Ordinary duties that hold good universally, suggested Ambrose, should be called the simple, elementary *commandments*. But what Cicero called the "perfect" duties that one cannot impose on everybody (the high ideals that the average man cannot reach), were called by Ambrose *"evangelical advice."* The commandments hold good for everybody; the evangelical advice holds only for those who want to live a perfect life. This idea was later elaborated extensively in the "doctrine of perfection," a sub-division of Roman Catholic theological ethics.

In most cases, even in antiquity, doctrine followed life; life-practice precedes life-theory, and not the other way round as is popularly assumed. It was the age of the rise of monasticism. Many Christians could not manage to live according to God's will and to their conscience in everyday life. They partly withdrew from life and gave up many liberties in order to dedicate themselves to a life under the law of

186

perfection. Not everyone, however, could or would choose to do that. There were, and still are, other options, and I should like to mention a few here.

We must acknowledge the fact that we are sinful people, living in a sinful world. It is rather sad, but we cannot do anything to change that fact. We are bound to sin. Sometimes a person uses a white lie or a half-truth, or becomes a soldier and kills or tortures somebody. It is impossible not to sin consciously at some time. I once attended a Christian wedding-party that was opened with prayer. The man who led in prayer asked, in anticipation, for forgiveness of those sins that would be committed that evening. Presumably he knew they intended to drink too much.

There are a number of ways of dealing with sin. First, we have the Christian who says that being too narrow-minded, one simply gets nowhere; one must sin a little or else go to a cloister. We must inevitably go through life with dirty hands; the dirt can hardly be avoided.

Proponents of a second position try to soothe their conscience. They say that not everybody is compelled to live a perfect life. The Ten Commandments hold good for all people, but not the Sermon on the Mount. The latter applied only to the closest disciples of Jesus, who can be compared to the brothers and sisters from the cloisters. *They* can live purely, have everything in common, etc., but the "worldly Christian" need not live this way. God does not demand this perfection from *everybody*. God does not demand from the ordinary man more than he can do. He must try to live as well as possible, but if he does not succeed, then he has not committed a cardinal sin but a "daily" sin, an "imperfection." We need not have a guilty conscience about this imperfection. That applies only to the "deadly sins," not to the insignificant "daily sins." This is, of course, mainly a popular Roman Catholic idea.

A third attempt to solve this problem was offered by Luther. He proposed a "double moral," in the sense of a Christian and a civil moral. In his private life the Christian must be very strict. But in the life of secular ordinations, other laws and commandments are valid, and these other commandments are valid because God imposed them. In private life man is not allowed to kill, but as a soldier he may do just that. As a Christian one is free and not indebted to anyone, but as a citizen one is called to serve one's fellow-man.

St. Augustine once exaggerated by saying: love God and then do what you like. Similarly, Luther once said: believe in the forgiveness of sins and then sin bravely. Luther's advice was not as bad as it sounds. Luther considered God's grace to be so great and so deep that he thought of the "secular life" in the secular ordinations as a natural life on a far lower level than the spiritual life. Ours is a broken and sinful life and we must try to make something of it. We must be comforted by the gospel of forgiveness.

Here we have three conceptions that are different but still closely related. They are the predominant tendencies in Christian life and thought. Even Calvinism is still stamped in many respects by such conceptions. But Calvinism, and especially Neo-Calvinism, contain in themselves a possible way to conquer these problems in principle – not only in practice, but also in a scientific manner.

Reformed theology always denounced and fought these three conceptions in a fairly clear fashion. Their substitutes, however, were not always an improvement. Puritanism often degenerated into a new legalism, strengthened by a rationalistic exegesis. We see that Calvinism is now waning. What is left of it is reverting to the Lutheran way of thought as far as ethics is concerned.

This Lutheran way of thinking was arrested more than Calvinistic thought by pre-Reformational Roman Catholic thought. For this reason, orthodox theology (Reformed or Lutheran) has very little real resistance to modernism in the field of "social ethics," which is now strongly influenced by *socialism*, and no resistance to current Marxism and Neo-Marxism. It is rather distressing to realise that we can now expect little or no support from theological ethics or from orthodox theology in general against the growing domination of Christianity by socialistic thought.

Calvinistic philosophy, on the other hand, offers a wider perspective. This is evident in the areas of ethics and social ethics, because the task of theology is far more limited than that of philosophy.

Still, Christian philosophy cannot offer more than a perspective or an outlook, certainly not any clear-cut solutions for all practical life-problems. In fact, the pretension of theological ethics in all ages has proven to be false in this respect. If one takes theological ethics as a science, its pretension has always been to do what only a whole series of Christian special sciences can do. This becomes now even more obvious in the present developments in ethics.

Moreover, one must always consider that the task of every science is limited. Calvinistic philosophy offers no single guarantee for a Christian life in any sphere whatsoever. The same holds true for Christian theology. Calvinistic philosophy is only a *science*, and only in so far as it is a good science can it act as an *aid* to practical Christian life. In addition, as a *philosophy* it can only offer its assistance *indirectly*, because philosophy exercises its influence via the special sciences.

We must also remember that philosophy as scientific thought is necessarily an occupation at the surface or on the outside of life. It is theoretical thought, and theoretical thought is only *one expression* or one manifestation of life. Thought itself has deeper roots but, to the same extent that thought considers its own deeper roots, it also becomes less of a theory and more of a religious conviction and view of life.

190

On these deeper levels of life we obtain a view of the *"unity of life."* The total *life-attitude* becomes visible behind the great diversity of thought and actions in various spheres of life. All special problems of life are included in the question of the meaning of life. In man's self-reflection on the *meaning* of his existence, the depth of the human heart is revealed and the religious convictions lying at the bottom of the heart come to the surface.

From the beginning, Calvinistic philosophy pointed out the central place that should be allocated to the heart of man according to the Bible. Fundamental decisions, for better or for worse, originate in his heart, the source of all life. Because this is the case, the condition of our heart is vitally important. The Scriptures therefore command: guard your heart more than any treasure. In the heart we find the unity of life, which is the topic of our discussion. In our hearts we receive the guidance and influence of the Holy Spirit as we confront the data and circumstances of life. In this way we are guided in our obedience to the biblical message. In the heart the renewal of life has its human origin and its fertile soil. The seed of God's revelation in His Word and in the works of His hands falls in the fertile soil of the heart and germinates there. Both the seed of obedience and the seed of our disobedience to God's will (which is sown in our hearts by sinful and perverted life) are allowed to germinate.

This phenomenon can be expressed in the more

191

anthropological idiom by speaking of a personality centre, the "ego" as the core of the personality. The multiplicity of life, and all its incidental diversity, are focused on this "ego" as the centre of our life experience. This "ego" is responsible for the unity tendency in all diversity. Thus, the problem before us is this: how can the unity of life be manifested or expressed in the versatility and multiplicity of life?

In the versatile abundance of life, we distinguish between different social communities, life spheres or life sectors. Each life sector has its own character and task, its own responsibility, boundaries, and sphere of competence. We know, for example, that the state is not allowed to do everything in its power, even though it possesses a monopoly over the power of the sword. The church is not allowed to organise and control all life, not even under the cloak of its sole responsibility for preaching the Word of God and the fact that this Word claims man in his totality for the service of God. The same boundaries also apply to family life, schools, universities, trades, trade unions, political parties, sports, arts, etc.

Abraham Kuyper had a keen insight into this principle. He rightly formulated it as the fundamental principle of human society, using the convenient motto "sovereignty in the individual sphere." This implies a practical principle for the mutual relations between life-spheres, and for the limits of their competence.

This view of life and society was supported

and deepened by the philosophical theory of the diversity of modal aspects. This diversity is present in everything that God created, each according to its own character. In this theory the coherence between the different life-spheres is accounted for extensively, i.e., in the interwoven coherence which never contradicts the sovereignty in the individual sphere. Again, I should draw special attention to this final point, on account of misunderstanding that has arisen.

There is a great deal of coherence and interwovenness of different life-spheres, which results in various contacts, in cooperation and in common activities. Yet the internal individual character and competency of every life-sphere is left intact. The enduring characteristic nature and task of life-spheres brings about this coherence and cooperation without erasing any boundaries.

Marriage, family life, state, church, school, business – to name only a few important communities – now depend on one another to an even greater extent in our modern society. They cannot do without one another, yet they also cannot take over one another's task in a totalitarian way. To dominate another community is an ever-present danger which can only be countered by a fundamental conviction: God gave each of the different communities its own task and competency.

The philosophy of the Cosmonomic Idea stresses both the characteristic nature and task, and the mutual coherence and interwovenness, of different social structures. The fact that educational institutions and the church (in her preaching) are so involved in politics makes it necessary to examine this principle in greater detail. Both education and the preaching of the church must certainly be "socially relevant."

For more than a century the issue of social relevancy has been evident in art. Many people thought that literature, vocal and instrumental music, painting, and sculpture degenerated into a senseless glorification of forms if they did not serve "social consciousness." In the Middle Ages, art was subservient to the knowledge of faith and mystical religious ecstasy. Now, abstract ideals of beauty are on parole; we are to become *conscious of social criticism.*

It is evident that the particular task and responsibility of the different life-spheres do not seem to be satisfactory. We fear a fragmentary disintegration of life as it becomes divided into compartments. What is necessary is an integration, an inner coherence and unity in the direction of one's life. Hence the appreciation for spontaneity, for acting whole-heartedly as a complete human being.

People look for concise mottoes that can be applied consistently in all spheres of life. One of the demands of the spirit of our age is to level income, social status, competence, national borders, husband and wife, etc. As a result, the interference of the state in trade and even in science becomes more intensive day to day. Commerce aspires to political influence by means of its financial power. Because action groups outside parliament feel their interests are not properly represented by the members of parliament via the political parties, they loudly champion their demands.

As a result of their particular position, churches participate in breaking down boundaries. They nominate dozens of "councils," deputations, commissions to lead or "guide" many sectors of life (especially the political sphere), and they try to "influence" them in this way. The charity-boards of the church do not content themselves by relieving distress. Under Marxist influence they think they should also combat the social, structural, or political causes for distress. In the activities of the top councils of the church we see a totalitarian tendency similar to that witnessed in the Middle Ages. The congregation or the people of the church are continuously reproached because they are not active enough to follow this leading.

The same criticism applies to education in both primary and secondary schools. At present, universities are centres of political and social activities, rather than centres of science. These spheres vie with one another for supremacy. Must science take the lead in all spheres, or should social and political developments control science and make it subservient to their aims?

We discern the imperative and legitimate summons to live from *one* ethos, one central basic attitude, one view of life, one simple and all-encompassing deep inspiration. The Calvinists and Communists reveal this summons most clearly. Various forms of humanism also seek this inspiration and integration of the diversity of life in a less explicit but still active way. In the chaotic diversity and immensity of life, we seek an outlook and grip on life. But there are many views on the unity of life, and they all compete with one another.

Science and scientific technique dominated our culture for centuries. But in the present struggle for supremacy between science and ideology (or the view of life), the latter claims its natural but suppressed rights. This claim is very important because it gives a deeper seriousness and meaning to our lives than the competition between different life spheres, which in principle are equal to one another. In so far as modern man is inclined to surrender himself totally and internally to an inspiring *life-ideal*, our age is looking for a deeper motivational level.

Formally this search is welcomed, because God created man to live with "heart and soul," giving himself totally to his all-encompassing ideal of life. The situation becomes pathetic when this ideal is not the will of God and service in His kingdom. The life-ideal and inspiring unity of our life is the fundamental deification of only one or two possibilities; the total absolutizing of politics or economy, of prosperity or pleasure.

Thus, the distinct character and particular responsibility of every life-sector must be fully recognised and be maintained practically. Our age rightly demands a new emphasis on the spiritual coherence of the different expressions of life. I should like to illustrate this formal conclusion by way of a few examples.

Education is an important sector of our society, and teachers should be competent in their subjects. If Christian education naturally is to prepare pupils and students for their social functions, however, it should be adapted to the diversity of life. The Christian school should not only require that teachers be competent in their subjects, but also that they have a positive attitude to life. This *attitude to life* or *ethos* is important for two reasons. In the first place, the tie between concrete expressions of life and one's total attitude toward life is fundamental. And in the second place, the spiritual enemies of Christ's kingdom cunningly formalise faith and politics on the one hand and competence in a profession on the other hand.

Modern man is now inspired emotionally far more than before by ideals and fundamental convictions. He has a need to make spontaneous and concrete decisions when confronted with such social phenomena as poverty and wealth, fidelity in marriage and divorce, normal and abnormal sexuality, authority, war and peace, increase and security of prosperity, progressiveness and conservatism, etc. To speak of labour, for example, as if it does not fall within the realm of social structures, is now thought

197

to be a formalistic abstraction. We also understand better how social structures are also founded in more profound attitudes of life and ultimately in basic motivations.

If education aims to prepare children for life, then it should strive to know the spiritual coherence between concrete sectors and events of practical life. Because this challenge requires more than competency in a certain subject and in technique, an educational institution should know whether its staff is able to convey the spiritual and ideological coherence of the phenomena of life. Christian educators obviously understood this principle better in the past. Now the Marxists understand this need better than the Christians. The Marxists place the different facts and processes of life within the framework of the class warfare between possessors and exploiters, between rich and poor, between capitalists and the suppressed masses of exploited people. In this perspective all life is experienced and judged and, by adopting this attitude, all life easily obtains an economic-political flavour.

For Christians this situation should be different. They acknowledge that faith may not be isolated and formalised because of the unity of life and the unity of God's law. Its effects should be expressed in concrete decisions in various life-spheres. Christian education must cover the whole domain of human life, because this is exactly the kingdom where God must be served as King and Redeemer.

We must often speak and decide on social and political issues, but our opinions must necessarily be related to our fundamental choice to serve God. The criterion for being a Christian does not lie in the practical decisions as such. Concrete decisions can be influenced negatively by diverse circumstances like customs and traditions, of which one is not really aware. Consider also the influence of public opinion and the misinformation offered by the mass media, which are seldom led by a radically Christian inspiration. Consider the leadership of people who are erroneously followed in good faith. In all these realms the spirit of the world or the spirit of the Anti-Christ is active.

It is possible, therefore, that a mistaken decision in some sphere of life can be in conflict with the fundamental Christian decision of surrendering one's heart to Christ. Apart from being an inconsistency on the side of the Christian, such a wrong decision can also be symptomatic of a religious falling away from Christ, of not belonging to Christ and of not being guided by the Holy Spirit. We can never judge, however, if this is the case for our fellow human beings. We should be careful not to place ourselves on the tribunal of God in order to pronounce an absolute verdict on somebody else. Only God knows the hearts of people and can judge the spirits.

The conversation between the leading powers in education (parents, school committees, principals) and the teachers should be conducted in all frankness, caution, love, and patience. These qualities should be evident when principals are interviewing applicants, when parents and teachers meet for discussions and when educators gather for annual meetings. The heart of the matter should always be an awareness that Christian teaching is an extension of Christian education.

If, in specific cases, a fundamental decision is neglected because people have taken an inconsistent position in social and political issues, then the particular character of the Christian teaching techniques will have to be tested in each individual case. Are they obsolete? Do they perhaps cause some damage? The spiritual climate of a certain period should also be considered, and also whether an incidental case could later become a dangerous precedent. For this reason, I want to mention another point here.

There is a second reason why it is important to know the implication of the Christian ethos – the spiritual struggle between the kingdom of Christ and its adversaries. In this struggle, old stratagems are applied. As long as spiritual enemies do not have the upper hand, they use camouflage and other stratagems. The opportunistic, tactical accommodations usually maintain "long-term objectives." I am referring specifically to the ease of the abstract formalising of principles, confessions, starting points and objectives. Once more, contact is suddenly sought with the diversity of life. For the point of view of diversity, it is said that the school must remain objective, science must remain neutral, the church must not interfere with everything, and politics is a case of personal free conviction which may never be used to irritate anybody in a non-political sphere.

Yet this is a very dangerous stratagem. Many Christian institutions, even churches, were wrecked by this formalised faith-life. The endorsement of a particular principle is severed from one's total life attitude and is thus abstracted functionally and formalised. This is unnatural and contrary to nature. Sometimes one realises that a certain ecclesiastical opinion also has an effect outside ecclesiastical life. Marxists thus realise the overtures of the political meaning of socialism for education, the army, police, and judicature, and they aspire to many functions occupied by political, congenial spirits. A religious conviction to the Christian is more and more a political conviction to the non-Christian. But this is clearly a stratagem for the sake of infiltration.

Humanistic liberalism previously claimed that the only guarantee for scientific objectivity and reliability was public and "neutral" education. In the same way, socialistic humanism finds the guarantee for social justice and the liberation of man only in socialistic organisations and socialistic life attitudes or basic attitudes.

We spoke earlier about the importance of recognising and knowing the human ethos, the basic spiritual attitude. To a certain extent this ethos consistently influences our daily life. We also spoke about the tie between the different expressions of life on the outside or upper layer of our lives and the deeper layer of our existence, converging in the heart. The recognition of the tie must not lead us to disregard the relative independence of different sectors involved in specific acts. On the one hand, there is sovereignty in the individual sphere – the distinctive responsibility of different communities. On the other hand, we have the coherence and inner connection between diverse life expressions at a deeper level. A certain unity of life-style can be observed in an individual's character through his actions in various spheres. In the same way a common ethos of a spiritual community manifests a spiritual affinity between people and activities in various life-spheres.

The organisational splitting up of schools, political parties, radio and TV associations, social aid organisations, etc., is more than just an ideal to be welcomed or rejected. In the first place it is a given fact; this splitting is evident long before it has any organisational power. Spiritual groups manifest themselves and exert influence. Their spiritual power leads to separate organisations. This splitting up is a legitimate organisational specialisation true to human reality. An inner and deeper life dimension is dynamically active under the surface of human life, inspiring human life spiritually and giving direction. The whole human personality and the whole of society are therefore involved in the activities derived from this inner life dimension.

I still want to draw attention to some practical consequences because we err in two ways if we emphasise one of the two sides of the same truth. First, we can lose sight of the sovereignty or distinctive character and responsibility of diverse spheres of life, in which case the boundaries fade away, are ignored, or wiped out. Inevitably everything is then placed in the deeper, fundamental realm of one absolutized sphere of life. Life is expressed in terms of either church or politics, or is reduced to the denominator of pleasure-seeking, science, sport, or economic welfare. Such an idol knows no limits; it is absolute and totalitarian in its demands.

When we are confronted with the politicising of education, of the preaching of the church or of trade, it is pointless to deny that the school, the church, or trade has something to do with politics. School, church, and trade cannot act as if they are politically or religiously neutral. The church has her own typical ecclesiastical responsibility toward politics in proclaiming the central principles for political life from the Word of God. The task of rulers is to practise law and justice on earth, and the task of citizens is to assist rulers, under the leadership of the authorities, in executing their charges. What this implies in specific detail is, as a rule, not an issue to be judged by the churches, schools, or commerce. Schools should teach children the structure of society and its divisions, so that they can learn to differentiate what is manifested in society as a whole and in its diverse communities.

Political preaching is no substitute for the ideal of non-political preaching, but the preaching should speak from the Word of God about the unity of life and the one Holy Ghost that lives in the versatile body. Sovereignty in the individual sphere must be recognised but must never lead to division of life in isolated compartments. The *distinction* is very necessary, but it must never be over-emphasised in a theoretical, formalistic *separation*.

A great deal could be accomplished if young people in Christian schools could be taught to resist the tendency to judge life from the one-sided view of a political ideology. In the face of all kinds of totalitarian tendencies, future generations will have to fight certain tendencies. In confronting the "doctrine of society," for example, they will have to be aware of the undifferentiated use of general slogans. For example, "human equality as a directing principle for public life" must be countered. Similarly, people will have to confront the mythology of abstract human rights separated from history, and the historical process of forming judicature nationally and internationally.

Moreover, a Christian doctrine of society should train youth in the struggle against the relativistic view of society. The latter interprets morals, marriages, families, states, business, and churches as nothing but human creations, of which the basic structures are changed or cancelled according to the needs of the present moment. The Christian doctrine of society

204

will have to unmask the myth of self-realisation, the passion for emancipation, or the unrestrained ideal to democratise life.

All of these examples relate to our insight into the distinctive nature and responsibility of the different social communities. Here I am referring to "sovereignty in the individual sphere," which is rooted in God's pluriform creation of all things "to their nature." This abundance of creation is self-evident to anyone who looks at reality. If this abundance of creation is ignored, it is revenged in history.

Given the inevitable concentration and integration of human life, the question of a *true* or a *false* integration of life still remains. Integration is a fact and a task, a "normative fact" as some sociologists would call it. Integration refers to serving God totally and in every sphere of His kingdom. In the case of a false integration, we see the substitute of another religion and a totally different direction of life. But this is not religious neutrality, nor is it a negation of religion. This is simply another *ethos*.

In the depth of the ethos of the human being lies the real ground of integration in which the unity of life is rooted. This is a spiritual depth-level, where the great spiritual contrasts in life are embodied in religious convictions and life-attitudes. If we fail to look in the human heart for the deeper unity and coherence of our different actions in the diverse sectors of society, we inevitably look for it in *the wrong places*. Then we are led astray by the reality of the many cross-connections. Involuntarily one life-sector is considered to be of much more importance than another. We are tempted to absolutize one sector in such a way that we attach an absolute and integral meaning to it (which in fact can be granted only to the human heart).

The spiritual antithesis can, therefore, neither be denied nor cancelled. It is also a fact – a religious motivating power which brings about spiritual conflict. The antithesis is found in specific decisions we make in various life-spheres. It is found primarily in the heart of man and in his fundamental choice of life-attitude, his ethos. According to the divine plan for the structure of human action, the deep spiritual unity of human life has more meaning than the multi-coloured diversity in various functions and spheres.

A fitting metaphor would be that of the sun and the light radiating from it. Sun and light are indissolubly one. There is no light without sun and no sun without light. Just as we distinguish between light and the source of light, we can also distinguish between life and the source of life. We should persevere in looking for the source of life in the surrender of our hearts to the real Source and Creator of both heart and life.

CHAPTER 9

Ethos – an Historical Study

DR. SCHIPPERS' INAUGURAL speech as professor in 1950 was a lecture on "The Sources of an Ecumenical Ethos." Only a few years later, in 1954, his book on "The Reformed Moral" appeared. In this chapter we want to consider these two nouns: Ethos and moral. Schippers necessarily had to be brief in his oration and only indicated by "a single word" what is to be understood by "ethos;" on the other hand he elaborated extensively in his book on the nature of "morals." Here, however, we shall discuss "morals" briefly and have a closer look at the nature, place and meaning of "ethos" as a main theme.

In philosophical ethics, also called "practical philosophy," ἔθος or ἦθος has been under discussion from early times. In many descriptions of the history of ethics we are reminded of the now very familiar fragment 119 of Heraclitus: ἦθος ἀνθρωπω δαίμων. Heidegger and Jaspers and many others wrote commentaries on this and also expressed their interpretations in rather diverging translations.

Perhaps one can learn more of Heidegger's

207

philosophy in his translation than of the view of Heraclitus. Nevertheless, it is important to take notice of his interpretive translation of the above-mentioned fragment: "Der (geheure) Aufenthalt ist dem Menschen das Offene für die Anwesung Gottes (des Ungeheuren)."[30] Heidegger gives a detailed argumentation of this translation and dismisses the usual conception of ήθος as the "Eigenart" of man. He does not mention Jaspers, who offers the following translation: "Sein Ethos (sein Wesensart) is dem Menschen sein Dämon." I shall return to this statement presently.

Jaspers' view of ήθος is closer to the current one. The usual views, according to Heidegger, are modern conceptions, not those stemming from the Greeks. To Heidegger the word ήθος means sojourn, abode.[31] For this interpretation, according to various dictionaries, he could appeal to diverse classical writers, including Homer (Odyssey 14, 141 and Iliad 6, 511) and Hesiod (Erga 222). The latter already derived the more current meaning of attitude, custom, moral from the original meaning (Theog. 67).[32]

The relation with what is δαίμων must also be considered. The ethos (whatever it may be) is to man a δαίμων. Even outside the context of the already quoted "translation," Heidegger interprets this passage as follows: man stays, in so far as he is human, in the vicinity of the god (ibid. 39). To support this

---

30. M. Heidegger; *Brief über den "Humanismus,"* Bern 1947, 41.
31. M. Heidegger; *ibid.*, 39.
32. H. Reiner, article *Ethos*, HWP 2, 1972, 813.

view, he refers to a story of Aristotle on Heraclitus and adds his own extensive story (challenged by J. Mansveld), resulting in the translation quoted above.

In the highly commended translation of Heidegger's publication in Dutch, Heidegger's conception of the three words of Heraclitus then reads: "The (familiar) sojourn of man is the openness before the face of the god (of the non-familiar)."[33] Heidegger links this with the idea that the original ethics is the reflection on the common daily sojourn of man, "the reflection that considers the truth of Being as the original element of man as an existing being" (loc. cit.).

We are struck by the accent in Heidegger's view on the "original element" of man, the "truth of Being." Do we have an echo here of the view we meet in the circle of the Stoa via the anthology of Stobeus?[34] They regard ethos as the *source* of human life: ἦθος ἐστι πηγη βίου, like the omnipresent rational godhead who is also called δαίμων. Whatever Heidegger's view, Jaspers calls the fragment of Heraclitus an "ergreifende Satz" in that part of his work on the great philosophers which he names "Aus dem Ursprung denkende Metaphysiker." To Jaspers this "ergreifende" does not seem to lie in a new

---

33. M. Heidegger, *Brief over het "humanisme,"* translated by G. H. Buyssen, Tielt-Utrecht 1973, 67. In this translation a post-script by Dr. J. Mansfeld inter alia on Heidegger's and Aristotle's interpretation of the fragment of Heraclitus, see 129.

34. Stobeus, *Eclogae physicae et ethicae*, ed. Steineke 1860 - 1864, II, 6, 36.

understanding of ἦθος but in the addition of δαίμων. According to Jaspers this means that ethics is more than a purely natural datum: "es ist Nicht der Damon als ich selbst der ich eigentlich bin und der ich mich noch nicht als solchen kenne und weiss."[35]

It is always difficult to interpret accurately a single fragment of three words, particularly if these are the words of "the obscurant of Ephesus." If one reads the various technical and authoritative commentaries and translations, a clear impression emerges. In the conclusion (and even the inception) of H. Reiner's article on "Ethos" in the HWP, this impression is reduced to a purely psychological and sociological interpretation.

Reiner is correct if he summarises the term "ethos" by expressions such as attitude, disposition, moral character, moral customs, etc. Since the last part of the nineteenth century, this term has been restricted to the denotation: "bleibende Gesinnung und Haltung eines Einzelnen oder einer Gemeinschaft."[36] But then the "ergreifende" idea of Heraclitus is lost. Presumably Heidegger and Jaspers would protest against this, and we, from other motives and from another ground-motive, would protest with them. With the "Aus dem Ursprung denkende Metaphysiker" a consciousness still remains of this "mehr" than the natural in the ethos, to which the

---

35. K. Jaspers, *Die grossen Philosophen*, Vol. I, Sonderausgabe des Abschnitts *Aus dem Ursprung denkende Metaphysiker*, München 1957, 30.

36. H. Reiner, *ibid.*, 815.

word δαίμων of Heraclitus refers.

We would definitely express ourselves differently; we say that what is understood by the metaphysical origin-thinkers as "mehr" is "purely natural." Wilhelm Capelle translates δαίμων as "Schicksal."[37] Perhaps this term is nearest to the intention of Heraclitus, but who could tell? This term refers to God's dispensation of providence in human life, although "Schicksal" makes a caricature of it. It concerns a guidance that is not "heteronomous determination" but is present in human existence as "das Offence" (Heidegger) – the possibility, the point of contact. Moreover, behind this presumption of the depth of the human ethos lies a reference to the function of a source, a πηγη (the Stoa), from which the (whole) human life is nourished πηγη βίου (see note 5).

As Western idolatry of thought emerges more clearly in the process "Vom Mythos zum Logos" (W. Nestlé), human self-knowledge fades away. By the time of Plato, we are already on the level of the apparently uprooted "Logos." To Plato the ήθος as the inner, deepest life-attitude – is brought about by two factors: διάθεσις (or "Psychosomatic") state of the natural dispositions and έθος the customs and virtues acquired through habituation, training, and

---

37. W. Capelle, *Die Vorsokratiker*, Stuttgart 1968, 156: "Dem Menschen ist sein Wesen sein Schicksal." In a footnote Capelle adds: "Treffend hiezu Diels in der Sonderausgabe: ήθος *ist die aufsich selbst beruhende Art* des Charakters und Denkens: die 'Individualität'" (my italics).

adaptation.[38] Among those whose deformed faith (the "mythical consciousness") has not been totally reasoned away, there still resounds an echo of the more penetrating view of Heraclitus. In a similar way Socrates, Plato and Aristotle sought the meaning of life in their conception of εὐδαιμονια.

However, we must not translate this too easily into "happiness." Kerford rightly calls attention to this temptation. "But if we have to be more explicit as to what eudaimonia involves, we will say that the good for many is the fulfilment of his function;" with Aristotle, the actuality of the soul in relation to its function.[39] This idea contains more than happiness. In εὐδαιμονια we again meet the δαίμων, the good, higher power that has good intentions for human beings and motivates them deeply. This motivation is not only taken as a causa finalis – a far removed ultimate ideal and the ultimate ideal of blessedness – but as a driving force coming from the origin and sustaining ground itself. This ground is present in various actions, in every occupation or function, which *has* the τέλος originally *in* itself (ἐν-τελέχεια).

An identification of meaning is going on in the continuous combining and blending of ἦθος, ἔθος, εὐ ζῆν, εὐ πράττειν and εὐδαιμονια. In other words, the fragment of Heraclitus remains interesting: ἦθος ἀνθρώπως δαίμων.

Since the time of Plato (Νομοι), different writers

30. Plato, Νομοι, XII, 968 d
39. G. B. Kerford, *Aristotle*, in Paul Edwards (ed.) *The Encyclopedia of Philosophy* I, New York-London 1972, 161.

have tried to fix the continuous combination and shifting of the words ἦθος and ἔθος. This attempt was evident in three different "Models." First, ἦθος and ἔθος were differentiated as the more inner attitude, in contrast to the more outer practice, legislation, custom, cult or moral. The greater constancy and firmness of the ἦθος was compared with more fluctuating and individual customs. Finally, these thoughts were often accompanied by the indiction of different levels and a difference in depth. Thus, terms like ground-attitude, ground-motive and basic disposition came into use. (We have already drawn attention to the πηγη of the Stoics.)

These changes are not common in modern usage. We easily speak of somebody's "deepest" motives, or of "deeper" motives in comparison with arguments, motives, customs, practices, etc., lying closer to the surface. Meanwhile, "ethics" as the theoretical reflection on the "ethos" ran parallel to the development of philosophy and the various special sciences.

The traditional interpretation of the development from "Mythos" to "Logos" was in fact a pre-Christian denial of the gods, a secularisation.[40] This denial was consummated in the diversion from traditional tribal gods and the myths evolving from the derailed faith-phantasy concerning the gods. Man preferred *other gods*, namely "Logos" – "reason." This way the view on ethos was made secular, horizontal, social and psychological.

40. Plato, Νομοι, XII, 968 d.

213

In the medieval doctrine on conscience, something still remained of the "mehr" which Heidegger and Jaspers spoke about in reference to fragment 119 of Heraclitus. Moreover, there were persistent biblical influences in scholastic ethics, and in the doctrine of the conscience-basis (συντήρησις or συνείδησις). As a result, a certain open-mindedness was maintained for the supra-natural revelation of at least the first and evident principles of moral law in the rational nature of man: "das Offene für die Anwesung Gottes."

Meanwhile the philosophical-anthropological contents moved to moral theology. Of the three mutually blending viewpoints of all ethics indicated by Schleiermacher – the doctrine of good, duties, and virtues – the first two were absorbed during our time in the philosophy of values and the latter in psychology. O. F. Bollnow deems it fruitless to make the effort to delineate ethics from psychology.[41] Indeed, "psychology" in our time is considered identical with "doctrine of personality"[42] or identical with knowledge of character,[43] and the norms from

41. O. F. Bollnow, *Wesen und Wandel der Tugenden*, Frankfurt/M 1958, 20:
   "Phychologie und Ethik sind als Gegenstandsbereiche gar nicht mehr gegeneinander abzugrenzen; ihre Gebiete überschneiden sich zu weiten Teilen, und der Unterschied liegt nur in der Fragestellung, mit der sie an ihren Gegenstand herangehen, und diese geht, wenn auch spezifisch verschieden in der Blickweise, doch zugleich immer auf den ganzen Menschen."

42. Ph. Lersch, *Algemeine psychologie*, original title: *Aufbau der Person.*

43. P. Helwig, *Charakterologie*, Stuttgart 1957. ". . . characterolo-

created and experienced reality are sometimes banned to the "higher spheres" of the domain of values or of biblical commandments.

Here a relatively new plant is grown in the old soil of the dualistic ground motive of nature and freedom, nature and spirit, world and church. This dualism manifests itself, in spite of all "holistic" efforts to an "einheitliche" cultural anthropology, as an almost unconquerable power. Classical and medieval thought (with its form-matter scheme) took this power up in itself, and its presence continues in a modern way. When life and/or thought are severed from their root in the real Origin and unity in Christ, then they are inevitably split in an inner antinomical dialectic.

Within these modern realms of thought, the reality of ethos as a problem keeps thrusting itself on theoretical thought. The original metaphor of a depth-dimension of life – which is stronger than what is at the surface and manifests a converging concentration of the relation of God's revelation to His will – is totally secularised. The "Tiefenperson" who was introduced by F. Krauss in 1919 in psychology, and which also distinguishes four Schichten, now figures as "endothyme ground,"

gy isn't any part of the domain of general psychology. The domain of characterology is the same as that of psychology, but then determined from a particular view-point .
. . The problem to delimit characterology from general psychology lies in the fact that in the end all psychic life . .
. can be apprehended from this viewpoint."
Dutch translation: Aula, 92, 14.

as sub-structure under the rational superstructure of the "Kortikalperson." In general, man can understand the psychological Schichtenlehre (which in the footsteps of N. Hartmann and E. Rothacker was developed into different variants) as primarily a radical secularisation of anthropological thought. The same must be said of its chief American counterpoints, e.g., A. R. Gilbert's idea of the human person as "Intentionalitätsgefüge,"[44] or of the newest resignation, which makes a virtue of the problem that man cannot realise an idea about the unity of man.

In an almost *rancorous* aversion[45] to all-encompassing "thought-systems," man advances on "empirical" grounds, supported by much conflict-psychology, the apparently "modest" idea of the essentially contradictory human being.[46] The philosophy of Dooyeweerd however, was a radically reformational turn in scientific thought. It implied the traditional problem of ethos in the doctrine of the four ground-motives of the development of

---

44. A. R. Gilbert, *Recent Theories of Stratification of Personality*, in: JPs 31, (1951), 3 – 19 and id., Seelenlebe und Menschenbild, in *Festschrift zum 60 Geburtstag von Philipp Lersch*, München 1953, 43-51. Both publications reprinted in: N. Petrilowitsch. *Beiträge zur Psychologie der Persönlichkeit*, Darmstadt 1967, 310 – 344.

45. O. F. Bollnow, *Die philosophische Anthropologie und ihre methodischen Prinzipien*, in R. Rocek und O, Schatz, *Philosophische Anthropologie heute*, München 1972, 36.

46. II. R. Lückert, *Der Mensch, das Konfliktträchtige Wesen. Das Konzept vom Menschen in der gegenwärtigen Psychologie*, München (1972).

Western culture.[47] After further consideration of this doctrine, it becomes clear that in the last instance the term "ground" is taken seriously; there is only *one* ground-motive, namely God's revelation of His will in creation and redemption.[48]

In opposition to this position the counter-force of religious apostasy, which is unfathomable in origin, manifests itself as the ground-motivation of life during and after the fall. In the different "Kultur-kreise," and over the course of centuries, this ground-motive acquired a number of typical historically founded configurations. Of these Dooyeweerd mentions three: the Graeco-Roman ground-motive of form and matter, the synthetical motive of nature and supra-nature, and the humanistic ground-motive of nature and freedom.

In these few catch words the widely encompassing and profound doctrine of religious ground-motives has only been partially indicated. We must still do a lot of investigation to see if this doctrine of ground-motives can be maintained in its present and preliminary form. A more nuance-filled elaboration is necessary and should be developed in "philosophical ethics."

The great benefit, the "Vorstoss im Neuland" which Dooyeweerd presented here, leads us out of the impasses of traditional ethics.

---

47. H. Dooyeweerd, *Reformatie en Scholastiek in de wijsbegeerte*, Vol. 1 Het Griekse voorspel, Franeker 1949, 17–64.
48. Cf. also J. P. A. Mekkes, *Grondmotief*, in Phil. Ref (1966), 122.

The fusing of ethics, cultural anthropology, psychology, doctrine of personality and social criticism that is considered necessary in our times does not solve the problem of the impasses in a consistent view, but rather manifests its disorderly and contradictory "angles of incidence" more clearly (see note 17). The methodological idea of different "angles of incidence" only camouflages the lack of a vision on the structural unity of the sciences.

Modern ethics, often understood as a doctrine of the motivations of human conduct,[49] thus actually approaches psychology, from which it cannot delimit itself sensibly anymore according to O. F. Bollnow (see note 12). On the contrary "critical" psychology approaches ethics[50] more closely. From the factual development of diverse sciences, the inner convergence-tendency of the sciences cannot be denied any longer. The Erlanger school of Lorenzen, Schwemmer, Kamlah, and others[51] developed a vision of the inner unity of ethics and philosophical anthropology, and in this instance their view of anthropological pedagogics and pedagogical anthropology converges.[52]

---

49. Cf. e.g., H. H. Schrey, *Einführung in die Ethik*, Darmstadt 1972, 19 – 21.

50. Cf. various contributions in Hans Thomae, *Die Motivation menschlichen Handelns*, Köhl-Berlin 1965, 1966.

51. P. Lorenzen, *Normative Logic and Ethics*, Mannheim, 1969. O. Schwemmer, *Philosophie der Praxis*, Frankfurt/M 1971. W. Kamlah *Philosophische Anthropologie, Sprachliche Grundlegang und Ethik*, Mannheim 1973.

52. Cf. W. Loch, *Die anthropologische, Dimension der Pädagogik*

In its published form, the philosophy of Dooyeweerd contains parts, chapters, and paragraphs, but in its philosophical vision it is a unity, making a study of separate parts impossible. From beginning till end, the broadly developed cosmology is anthropologically fitted into the framework of the central life-view and anthropological view of this philosophy. This central vision is the insight into the time-transcending "root" of human existence, its participation in Christ who is the sustaining Ground and Truth of all reality. This is the key to the understanding of this new vision about created reality.[53] It concerns a vision of a real victory over dualistic thought, which actually, dispositionally, and ethico-religiously rules Western science.

The whole complex problem of motivations of human actions is reduced by the philosophy of the Cosmonomic Idea to its transcendent basic denominator without reducing one time-aspect to another. Only in this way is it possible to recognise the different depth levels in human motivations, with their particular meanings and ranges.

These depth-differences can only indirectly be joined to what Lersch and others call the "endothyme

(NPädB, 1–2), Essen 1963; A. Flitner, and others *Wegen zur pädagogischen Anthropologie*, Heidelberg 1967; O. F. Bollnow, *Die anthropologische Betrachtungsweise in der Pädagogik* (NPB 23), Essen 1968; and especially B. Gerner, *Einführung in die pädagogische Anthropologie*, Darmstadt 1974 (With an extensive bibliography).

53. H. Dooyeweerd, *De wijsbegeerte der wetsidee I*, Amsterdam 1935, VI.

ground" or the "Tiefenperson." This fundamentally functionalistic view, in which even an Ich-Schicht is mentioned (Rothacker), leaves us with a few insolvable problems, especially that of the possible mutual influence of these "Schichten." Often "mutual influence" is the last word on this problem, as if this is an empirical datum, making further inquiry impossible. Here we indeed touch the border area of scientific possibilities, although the border itself is not yet visible.

The complicated structure of human action forces us to use a very subtle dissecting knife in order not to "analyse" too crudely. Dooyeweerd carefully distinguishes the modalities of the individuality structures (of which the modalities are only aspects). He distinguishes four bodily structures, which are individuality-structures. All these are mutually interwoven into an enkaptic whole in which the individuality-structures found each other respectively. These are qualified respectively by the physico-chemical, the biotic and the sensitive modality, while the fourth one, the act-structure, has no fixed qualification.

In this act-structure I also distinguish the depth levels of the social and individual dispositions, and social and individual ethos. This ethos can best be compared to what Dooyeweerd calls ground-motives, even though we may definitely speak of a small but not unimportant difference of opinion in this respect. (It is unnecessary to expound on this issue

220

here. A preliminary outline of my view can be found in my dissertation, which I wrote under guidance of the present jubilaris.[54])

I would like to consider the theory of ethos in terms of Dooyeweerd's conception of intuition. I am surprised that he did not repeat his insights on intuition *mutatis mutandis* with regard to non-logical activities. On the other hand, and as a consequence of the above-mentioned omission, there is a need within the framework of Dooyeweerd's philosophy for a differentiation of depth-levels. I am thinking of instances when he simultaneously speaks of the religious driving force of the ground-motives in the transcendent centre of man (humanity). I would also mention clear religious-historically founded ground-motives which recur in specific centuries and slowly acquire a new configuration with many variants. Only that which takes place in time is accessible in its temporal appearance to theoretical examination. So the transcendent root of our religious choice of the heart is not accessible to philosophical judgement; only the temporal manifestation of this root in the motives, which in any case may still be called "ground" or "basic motives" in a temporal sense, is accessible.

The somewhat static metaphor of depth levels and level differences is just as traditional as it is one-sided and risky.[55] The metaphor concerns all human

---

54. A. Troost, *Casüïstiek en Situatie-ethiek*, Utrecht 1958, 372–384.

55. Cf. the many treatises in the technical literature on "*Schicht-enlehre.*"

life in temporal reality. In the case of the subject-side, the metaphor of "phases" would be more in place; to the law-side I feel justified to express myself in models we experience as more static, because this side concerns more or less constant structures. The degree of constancy, as far as the closer distinctions in the act-structure are concerned, depends on the depth-level *and* on how the act-structure is embedded and founded in the sub-structures of our temporal existence.

Thus we find on the level of individual disposition a "fixing point" where the act-structure is interlaced with the biotic and sensitive sub-structures of the body as totality.[56] This state of affairs is far more complicated than we could have indicated in the foregoing discussion. But we had to follow this line of thinking in order to accentuate the "depth" difference between moral and ethos. Morals, customs, character traits and aptitudes lie on the level or in the phase of dispositions. With regard to concrete acts and actions, they have a more continuous character.

From ancient times this issue was discussed in ethics in the "doctrine of virtues" due to the influence of Aristotle.

These virtues were seen as the continuous sediment of the actual exercises and repetitions, so that man realised the great importance of education and of people who can act as "examples," in addition

---

56. Cf. among others E. Kretschmer, *Körperbau und Charakter*, 1921, 1955.

to the importance of "institutions," social structures, etc.

From the start, the need for ease of survey meant that the division and summary of virtues (and skills) lacked the orientation scheme of modal qualifications of acts and actions. (These virtues, as dispositional and inchoative conditions, where intentionally directed toward such acts.) Both these objections (and others) can be raised against the traditional doctrine of virtues. In contrast, the philosophy of the Cosmonomic Idea opens the possibility of a deeper, more consistent, and more encompassing totality-view of man.

Regarding the first objection, Reformational philosophy brought about a fundamental change in our view of reality. It showed us the philosophical translation of an important biblical insight: the heart (soul, spirit) is the religious centre of our existence. Philosophically (i.e., from an inner scientific necessity) the heart was now seen in the light of the Scriptures as the transcending "ego," the religious concentration point of all human activities. In the heart, the disclosure of life directed to God (or away from God) has its origin and finds its direction in subjection to the cosmic law of divergence and disclosure. Stated differently, in subjection to the cosmic concentration-law of all life, including theoretical thought, the heart is again focused on its point of departure and origin.

Out of the confusion caused by the bewildering abundance of life, man comes to understand even further converging insights. In the end, and independent of his will, he comes to the necessary realisation that he was created *through God and for God*. By experiencing many personal and cultural-social dispositions, character-traits, and social structures, he is driven by the concentration law and subjective concentration-tendency to the discovery of his ground-attitude. In this way he reflects on the meaning of life. This life attitude is not called the "noetic super-structure" or the "endothyme ground" (Lersch), but the depth-layer of the ethos. The pre-theoretical consciousness of this depth-layer expresses itself in a practical, not systematic and complete, view of life. It always receives its seal from what one believes.

The second objection to the traditional doctrine of virtues is its inaccuracy and incompleteness. These faults can be corrected by a cosmological orientation to the modal "ways of existence" and to the functions of human life, qualified by their typical structures. This approach also includes a more critical look at social criticism and its infiltration in modern psychology.

The latter development led to the reduction of psychology to a sort of experimental neuro-physiology. This created the climate for a partly justified and holistically minded reaction in social criticism and social psychology. Psychology as characterology and theory of personality is in principle not able to resist the current Marxist ethos in its own

224

scientific field of research. For this purpose it lacks the insight into the range of the spiritual depth of the ethos. In this instance the anti-Marxist currents are also related to the Marxist in the way they both regard their secularised, pre-theoretical view of man.

Here we encounter only one configuration of the dynamic ethos that permeates and compels all life and thought from the inside. As a result, it is not unjustified to use terms like *spirit of the age* or *mentality* to indicate what we call ethos. Ethos is only treated in earnest when we see its temporary character – the way it is "preliminary." Not only do we see its structure as a temporal depth layer from which all life is "inspired" and dynamically driven, but we also recognise the beginning of "eternal rest" or the lack of it in the temporal, preliminary life. Such rest is evident not despite, but precisely *in*, all "changes of structure" and passing fashions.

CHAPTER 10

Ethos – A Systematic Introduction

The Term "Ethos"

IN OUR DEFINITION we usually prefer to call ethics "ethology." It comprises the depth-dimension of human action we can call the "ethos." Ethos is a term adapted from science and is in common usage in the scholarly community. But in everyday language the word loses its sharp definition. The term "ethos" must derive its exact meaning in our scientific usage from the "theory of personality."

It is still valuable, however, to consider expressions in colloquial language which are well known to everyone. These include attitude of life, fundamental attitude, spirit of the age, view of life, spiritual climate, mentality, basic disposition, inclination, etc. What matters most is our understanding of these terms as an indication of a basic motivational power, a fundamental motivation with some obvious characteristics.

The term "ethos" was originally a Greek word.

In Greek there is still a difference between èthos and éthos. This difference is comparable to (but not the same) as the difference in nature and depth suggested by us between ethos (èthos) and dispositions (éthos).

The Place of the Ethos in the Act-Structure

In the human act-structure we distinguish several depth layers or act-phases. Objectively viewed, we first see the external actions which are integrated with the inner *acts*. In the inner directedness to something and in our planning, we already anticipate in ourselves what we are going to do. This is the *intentional* character of our inner acts. Consciously or unconsciously, we direct our acts to normative points of view: norms, values, ideals, and goals.

In this context we must refer to dispositions – the deeper layer of our customs, morals, habits, thought-patterns, and ready knowledge found in our memory and in societal structures. In this depth-dimension of dispositions, our acts are conditionally determined. In this depth layer also lies the pattern for interweaving our whole act-structure into the non-normative substructures which are qualified sensitively, biotically, and physically.

"Under" these depth layers of the dispositions lies a basic layer of very deep motivations. In keeping with our geological figure of speech, these motivations form the deepest layer of our whole temporal existence, i.e., of our way of existence in the structures of the whole cosmic law-order. If we penetrate still deeper, we arrive at the "root" of our existence, our "heart," the personal centre, the "I," or whatever we wish to call it. Because of its time-character, we can, of course, form no concept of this root with our mental capacity. Stated differently, the ethos is the border area, the transition phase of our "I" in our concrete way of existence in time. It is the inner circle around the centre.

Some Characteristics of the Ethos

Thus we have determined the place of the ethos in the realm of the act-structure. It is the basic layer, border area and anthropologically (not chronologically) first phase of expression of our ego in our concrete existence. So we can go on to summarise a few characteristics of the ethos.

The Ethos as Motivation

This word, "motivation," is to be taken in the literal meaning found in its Latin origin. The Latin *moverse* means "put into motion, drive on," hence our words motion, motive, motivation, etc. Applied to our subject at hand, we can say that the human ethos is something that drives on *all* our actions, giving direction to them and urging them on.

But the ethos is to be seen *not only subjectively*, as for example when we speak of being motivated to a greater or lesser degree in our work. This facet belongs to ethos, but here we must also consider what motivates us *from the outside* – which can be almost anything. We often use the term "inspiration," which literally means "to blow in or inhale." In other words, something from the outside or from above comes *into* us and animates us, inspires us, drives us on. Thus the human ethos is a human inspiration both from the inside and from the outside. It is a motivation that seizes us and drives us on in a certain direction. As in everything else, we can distinguish a law-side and a subject-side in the ethos. In the following section, we will direct our attention mainly to the subject-side.

The Ethos as Fundamental Motivation and as Depth-Dimension

We know of many motives that start us off in a certain direction. A human being has passions and "cravings," manifested as dipsomania, hedonism, covetousness, and perverse ambitions. Passions and cravings like these are usually no more than dominant traits in our character, style of life and dispositions. They are not so fundamental that they become predominating. So covetousness or dipsomania, for example, can be combined with ambition or a thirst for knowledge and science, or with a desire for power and influence.

In the case of ethos, we have something wider in mind. The ethos is something that *groups together* all possible motivations and desires – something basic that *directs* all these impulses. The ethos has a totalitarian tendency in the sense that it determines the totality of our life, and not only one facet or sector, one function or one possibility. Hence we speak of a basic attitude, a ground motive.

But the latter term already refers to the supra-individual character of the ethos, because something that penetrates and motivates and directs our lives so fundamentally must necessarily manifest itself in our *society*. Humanity is not a collection of individuals that exists, like loose sand, as unconnected units. Therefore, the ethos is always associated with a social nature.

The Constancy of the Ethos

In connection with the anthropological depth of the ethos, and the use of "ground" as an adjective before "conduct" and "motive," we must also stress the relative consistency, continuity, and durability of the ethos. To this greater constancy is attached the metaphorical language of a *deeper level*. Just as water in the sea or in a river is more lively at the surface than in the deeper layers, so also is human life. Beneath the ever-changing activities there is a deeper dimension which is of a more continuous nature. The waves at the surface move in the direction determined by the wind, while in the depths the direction of the current or the total mass of water is constantly the same. In the same way the deeper direction of life manifests a certain constant ethos which is not visible in every activity at the surface, but still gives a certain direction to the totality of life.

The ethos is not totally invariable. Because of its depth and breadth it sometimes comprises centuries, groups of nations, and, individually, an entire human life. (If we undergo a religious "conversion," for example, this will bring a fundamental change into our lives.) Thus we can speak of the ethos of the cultures of the Middle Ages and of the Germanic Culture, and of Graeco-Roman ground-motives and those of modern Western man. The ethos comprises human lives, centuries, peoples, and continents.

Among other facets of life, science is constantly influenced by this ethos. The technique of acupuncture, for example, is almost unthinkable as a Western method of healing, just as are yoga techniques. This is why the philosophy of culture has always drawn the necessary connections between *culture and religion*. Therefore, we shall presently point out the primary characteristic of the ethos, namely its religious nature. But first we must pay attention to the social character of the ethos.

The Communal Character of the Ethos

The supra-individual nature of the ethos has been discussed already. It is a quality that penetrates our being to such an extent that it becomes of fundamental significance for all expressions of life, including the societal forms and relations of individuals. We therefore speak of "culture-ethos." By this we implicitly say that culture-ethos does not determine people as individuals but as a whole culture. We differentiate between Western cultures, Eastern cultures, and primitive cultures. Within these larger groupings we can still refer to cultural spheres (e.g., the Anglo-American, the West-European Continental, the

East-European, the South-European, the Semitic, the Central-Asiatic culture). In fact, Levy-Brühl even states that different cultures have a different logic.

We have also noted how the ethos is not the last word or the deepest dimension. The larger cultural spheres have not developed the character of their culture apart from their religion. We cannot conceive of Europe in its typical character apart from Christianity. We will return to this point in our discussion of the different types of ethos.

The Integrating Character of the Ethos

In the ethos we have a fundamental or basic attitude toward life, which also has an *integrating action*. Such integration is essential because the fullness and versatility of human life can easily confuse us. The possibilities for development are countless: the charm of possessions, the tasks to be done, functions to occupy, relations to share, ideals to strive after, etc. We can only realise a fraction of these aspirations in our lives.

Self-reflection from time to time saves us from nervous confusion. What do I want from my life? I must choose a path for my existence. I must try to distinguish between essentials and non-essentials. I must concentrate on the most important ends. For this introspection the German language uses the word "Sammlung:" we collect the data of our life *in the direction of a self-reflection.*

In this process we are trying to integrate our lives. We can compare this process to what happens in a funnel. The abundance on the whole circumference of the inside of the funnel flows together, converging at a deeper level. A similar concentration takes place in the direction of the heart of our existence.

Conversely, there is also a "flowing out" from the heart – the real point of departure for our life. This is where the crucial choice about the direction of life is made. Here our choice of life acquires the more concrete form of an integrated determination of position, a basic attitude of which we are conscious. To the extent to which the ethos is integrated and uncomplicated, it enforces itself by integrating, directing, and forming our dispositions and in orienting our concrete acts and actions. In the orienting function, the "religious-ethical" character of the ethos is concealed.

The "Religious-Ethical" Character of the Ethos

Most people are familiar with the term "religious-ethical." It seems to be a sensible word-combination. This expression suggests that the human ethos, as the deepest *proven* ground-attitude in individual and social life, has something to do with religion. Therefore, I prefer "ethos" to words like mentality, attitude, etc., because they have a meaning which lies nearer the surface. It is easier to work on a "change of mentality" or a charge of attitude than on a change of one's ethical-religious life-basis.

In this context I must also draw attention to the term "spirit of the age." What one calls "the spirit of the age" depends on what is believed by most people in a certain period (or, stated differently, is not believed, or is believed in a different way).

There is also a close connection between faith and ethos. Stated more accurately, the connection lies between the *contents* of *what* one believes and the fundamental life-attitude by which one lives and thinks. The dividing lines that manifest themselves in ethos and religion pass right through phenomena that lie at the surface. A certain faith can unite people who do not even understand each other's language, people who by their character cannot easily be held together, people of diverse ranks, classes, races, colours of skin and cultural levels. Through the ages, all great world religions manifested this religious-ethical unity which bridges all contrasts and thereby distinguishes itself from other types of ethos.

A disadvantage of the term "religious-ethical" is that the word "religious" is taken to qualify "ethical," and "ethical" is understood as a devotional phenomenon. Therefore, it will *not* be necessary to add "religious" because it fits in everywhere and is presupposed everywhere. Because of the total, all encompassing relation of God-man (cosmos), *all* existence is "religious" – our deeds, our knowledge, our dispositions, and our ethos. Man not merely *has* religion, he *is* religion. As a human being he stands in relation to his origin with the fulness of his life. For this reason, we can consistently use the adjective "religious" everywhere or nowhere. We generally use terms like devotional or faithful where common usage prefers "religious."

In any case, for the sake of intelligibility and by adapting ourselves somewhat, we make an exception in the case of the term "religious-ethical." As we stated earlier, the ethos lies in the border area of our existence and offers its first direct expressions in the form of our attitudes. Moreover, whenever we try to describe our ethos, we make pronouncements in which our faith is clearly manifested (regardless of what our religious direction may be). Usually we call the formulation of the contents of our ethos our "view of life."

Ethos and the View of Life

As a rule, man is to some extent conscious of his own attitude to life. Regardless, he should be conscious in any case. Self-reflection is an immanent feature of man, which can only be pushed aside by a forced "dispersal" in superficiality. "Dispersal" is the opposite of what was earlier called "Sammlung."

In common usage, dispersal is called the "intoxication" of life. But it is crudely superficial to call this "real life." Man does not come "to himself" anymore.

In various situations we spontaneously come to appreciations and judgements that betray our deepest attitude to life. As a rule, we confirm and justify our acts with thoughts and verdicts from our life-view.

For example, what counts is that we are happy; we are here to help one another; we are to serve and honour God with our whole life; our mission is to co-operate in the liberation and welfare of humanity. There are many examples worth mentioning. Such philosophical statements emanating from our life-view can refer to less than the whole of our life: to our view of love and marriage, the position of women in professional life, the task of a university, the desirability of a military power, of NATO, of what the churches are or should be, of the educational aims, etc.

Therefore, although our view of life can sometimes be a product of deeper reflection, it is definitely *not* a system and shows no *scientific-systematic character*. Our view of life is spontaneous, generally fragmentary, mostly formulated in incidental and immediate life-experience, and can often be traced in proverbs, sayings, and aphorisms.

Because the insights and statements pertaining to our life-view often refer to the crucial experiences of life (birth, suffering, happiness, destination, meaning, origin, etc.), it is conceivable that religious convictions soon manifest themselves in our view of life. To our mind, the view of life as a configuration of our attitude of life is guided by what we believe.

Our view of life, and the insights and opinions pertaining to it in separate life issues, is fully *practical*, interwoven with, and embedded in our actions. Therefore, ethos is our life-attitude toward the human law of life and toward the Giver thereof. Hence the expression in the previous section, namely "religious-ethical."

CHAPTER 11

Types of Ethos

IN WESTERN EUROPEAN culture we distinguish three main types of ethos, which can be described as southern and northern heathenism, Christianity, and post-Christian humanism. There are countless blends and cross-connections between these main types, and the main types can be sub-divided into numerous sub-types.

Before the commencement of our era, the Hellenistic form of Graeco-Roman civilization was evident in southern and central Europe and the Germanic/Teutonic culture in central and northern Europe. Both cultures were marked by a certain type of faith, namely the heathen faith. Naturally this faith can be distinguished in more detail in diverse sub-types of religions.

With the advent of Christianity in our culture (after a few centuries of battle for life and death between Christians and heathens), the Christian faith became dominant in the Western way of living and thinking. I intentionally said "dominant" and not "exclusive." From the start, Christianity existed in an

239

originally spontaneous and unintentional synthesis (blend) with heathenism, at the outset with Graeco-Roman culture and later with Germanic-Teutonic heathenism.

In the thousand years of the "Middle Ages," a *conscious synthesis* was evident in the way life was thought to contain a double order: a natural order and a supranatural order. Theologically, philosophically, and ethically this view was systematised in the scheme of *nature and grace*. Nature was the earthly, daily life with everything pertaining to it; supra-nature was the so-called spiritual order, comprising the grace of God, religion, the church, theology, the saints, and the miracles. In this synthesis these two "worlds," "orders," or "domains" were thought to be connected, so that nature could be a step or preamble to the supra-natural life in the domain of grace.

The subjective intention here was sincerely Christian. The ideal was that the whole life of Christians and of the Christian community should be biblical. But in theory and in practice the life and world view was strongly influenced by Greek philosophy. In its turn, Greek philosophy was totally unthinkable without reference to its religious root and its ethical attitude.

Roman Catholic theology and philosophy had the intention to Christianise "worldly" life with its nature-grace scheme, but the real result of this was an unintentional "de-Christianisation" of natural life. External natural life had to be subservient to church life, i.e., natural life had to be "baptised" by the church (cf. Catechism of Heidelberg XXVI, 72).

Instead of being made Christian, natural life remained un-Christian on both an individual and social level. The uncritical assimilation of traditional views on reality appears to have made Christianity vulnerable. Certainly this was the case when the spirit of the Renaissance and of Modern Humanism infiltrated Christianity during the 14th, 15th and 16th centuries. Obviously, there was an unconvincing biblical resistance, but no more than a traditional resistance born out of fear that the church might lose its power in society.

Humanism

About 1300 the inner decay of Christianity was so far advanced that the first synthesis had lost its vitality. The spirit of the Renaissance announced itself even though it was still mainly a movement in small elite circles of artists, kings, and scholars. A new era was on the way in European culture. People now started to dissociate themselves *more openly* from everything connected with power and authority – from kings, emperors, churches, priests, theologians, and even from God and His Word – the Bible.

The far-reaching identification of God and the Bible with the pope, church, priests, theology, power, and authority was one of the confusing factors in the whole issue. For this reason, the Reformation could sometimes hardly be distinguished from the

Renaissance. Practically, the Reformation was often confused with the Renaissance. Christian faith regarding redemption and liberation was interpreted in a *secularised* way; the terms remained, but the contents and meaning changed. The Renaissance was a spiritual "emancipation movement" in which man wished to be his own law-giver, "auto-nomous" (auto = self, nomos = law). The external bond between nature and grace gradually lost much of its scientific attention and slowly began to fade from daily life.

But humanism, even in its most radical and atheistic forms, was no simple repetition of heathenism. Humanism passed right through Christianity. This fact appears to have left a residue in our life-views. Pure humanism has an idea of freedom, which is a reversal or reflected image of the Christian idea of freedom. Freedom according to humanism is not lawlessness or anarchy. To humanism, freedom is auto-nomy, self-legislation through human reason (hypostatized at the expense of the human ego or selfhood).

Therefore, humanism could enter into a synthesis with Christian faith, because the tradition-bound individual could still make "room" for "religion," the Bible, etc. Man then decided for himself whether and to what extend he should believe in a so-called "Supreme Being." Man decided on his own what the rationally apprehended, inborn, moral nature of man contains as norms for action, etc. As a result, Europe has always struggled to sever itself from supernatural, metaphysical gods.

The Great Reformation

At the beginning of the 16th century, when the Renaissance was in full bloom and a new era dawned, there came into being a partial purification of Christendom in the movement of the great Reformation. The movement did not last long, however. Soon faith again functioned as if it were a supra-naturally filled ratio, and so faith-life became entangled in theology.

This scientification of faith – first orthodox but gradually encompassing more unorthodox elements – reached its culmination (or lowest point) in the period of the Enlightenment, the 18th century. The *radicalisation* of this secularisation process of Christian life and thought is now taking place in our age. Its beginning lies in the Renaissance (16th century), the second culmination point in the Enlightenment (18th century) and the radicalisation period in the middle of the 20th century.

Dialectics in Renaissance and Enlightenment Thought

The term dialectic is used here in the sense of an attempt to unite internally opposing attitudes of life. The humanistic ethos of the emancipated individual has radically cut the bond with God, and consequently man sees himself as self-legislator and self-redeemer. Within this humanistic ethos a tension still manifests itself, which was typified aptly by Kant in the

243

reputed tension between nature and freedom. I suggest a "reputed tension" because this dialectic rests on an incorrect, secular conception of both freedom and nature. But *within* the humanistic ethos this tension is still thorough.

After scientific development had made headway, the dialectical synthesis in the ethos manifested itself in the ideal of the free personality of *autonomous, emancipated man* on the one hand, and the *ideal of science* on the other hand. The ideal of science orients itself to the natural sciences. It intends to make science an instrument subservient to the emancipated and autonomous personality for the purpose of ruling nature *and* human culture and society. The connection between these two ideals appears to be dialectical, i.e., internally opposing. In modern times this connection is called by Hegel and later by Dooyeweerd and by Neo-Marxism the dialectics of the Enlightenment. More material on this subject can be found in *Dialektiek der verlichting* by J. Klapwijk.

The Modern, Christian Synthesis

In the new era, heralded by the Renaissance, both Roman Catholicism and Protestant Christian life and thought entered into a new synthesis. This is a second type of synthesis, namely the synthesis between the Christian life-attitude on the one hand and the modern dialectic mentioned above. Christianity no longer has any link with the heathen Graeco-Roman civilization as in the Middle Ages, but is linked instead with the humanistic civilization. For this reason, the second synthesis is complicated, because the ground-pattern of the first synthesis is still maintained. The dualism of nature and supra-nature, nature and grace, or the doctrine of the two domains (secular and spiritual) still remains. The difference, however, is that in the worldly domain of "natural earthly life" the ancient tension between a belief in fate and the longing for immortality (in philosophical terms: matter and form) does not disperse our thought. It is the modern humanistic tension of hypostatized *nature* and secularised *freedom* – the tension between the *ideal of science* and the autonomous emancipation-ideal of the *free personality* – that disperses our thought.

For this reason, Christians in the practice of science often go different ways. One looks for a synthesis with Neo-Positivist ideals of science, while the other looks for a synthesis with the emancipation-striving of the autonomous ideal of personality. This problem becomes evident in trends such as Personalism, Existentialism, and Neo-Marxism.

In both forms of synthesis, the Christian faith was fundamentally misinterpreted as if it were a "moral," or even a "moral system."

The Difference between the Medieval and Modern Synthesis

In contrast to the Middle Ages, it is not Christianity that "calls the tune" in this second synthesis, but humanism. Christianity is on the retreat in Western culture. The remnants beg for recognition and acceptance by following the alternating trends of the main types of humanistic ethos. In this way Christianity is involved in a struggle for life and death, while the main types of ethos fight for leadership in our Western culture – until an extra-scientific *military* power puts an end to this struggle.

CHAPTER 12

The Experience of Meaning as the Nucleus of the Ethos

Manifestations of the Ethos

BECAUSE THE ETHOS acts as a depth-dimension in human actions, the ethos manifests itself most clearly in the way people respond to the most fundamental issues of life. In principle the ethos governs all the expressions of our life, but it is hardly possible to illustrate this fact in all the small details of our everyday life.

The Three Principal Issues in the Meaning-Question

The ultimate issues – those that stand central in the whole of our temporary existence – are related to the *meaning* of our life. When we reflect on the meaning of human life, the theory of ethos should distinguish three major issues: the central questions of the *way of existence*; the questions concerning *origin*; and the question of *destination* in human existence.

These fundamental questions of life are not

247

always encountered in the form of conscious and clearly formulated questions. They force themselves on us in our self-experience and our experience of reality, so that sooner or later they become explicit in our minds. We encounter them in the *limiting-situations* and the ebb and flow of life, especially in those situations of deepest despair.

According to the level of development in our thought and speech, we formulate these questions more or less clearly. But in science, including philosophy, the clearest possible distinctions and formulations are necessary.

But we should not be deceived into taking these vital questions themselves to be theoretical and philosophical in nature. Not all questions are typical "problems" in the theoretical sense. Although "questions" and "problems" are used alternately in everyday speech, we should reserve "question" for practical life and "problem" for science. But we are accustomed to calling any vital question from practical life, to which there is hardly a clear response, a problem.

The above-mentioned "more fundamental issues of life," which concern the foundations and principal lines of our life, are soon seen to relate to life "in general." We then ask: what is the meaning of life (Leibniz, Heidegger)? What are we and our world heading toward? What do we want? How must we live? Of which beginning, principle, or development must our life be a continuation? Or in what direction must we change the course of events? Where do we come from and what are the implications of our history for the present and the future? In other words, there is no prospect for us without retrospection. The answers to all these questions are bound up in the meaning-question.

The Human Way/Mode/Manner of Existence

Judged from the viewpoint of our view of life and our philosophical view of reality, we can state that human existence manifests itself in the correlation between law-side and subject-side. The whole of philosophy, which is principally a theory of structure, exists in the analysis of the law-side of reality. It is precisely this reflection on the law-side of our cosmos, including questions about human existence, that inevitably leads to the question about the origin and nature of the law-side. Where does the law originate? What is its validity? In which direction does it actuate and motivate our life, and where does its propelling-power come from?

On the other hand, reflection on the subject-side of our cosmos, including human existence, inevitably leads to other questions. Where are we going, and for what end? What purpose does existence serve? What does man aspire to? Thus, a reflection on our concrete way of existence raises the fundamental question of whence and whither – the questions of origin and destination.

But philosophy as a theory of structure has

no answer to these questions. Philosophy will inevitably face these questions, but philosophy itself can give no answer to them. They are the so-called "transcendental" questions, i.e., questions directed to the transcendence, from whence no direct answer to our theoretical questions is possible.

Questions Concerning the Origin

The term "origin" already has two meanings: as concept and as idea. As concept, every question concerning the origin is bound to the causality relation. The concept origin is then understood as cause, and as such it always has the moment of the physical analogy. When this concept cause is related to reality as a whole, it transcends reality. The cause of reality cannot itself be reality: otherwise, the concept cause would fall away completely.

In the philosophical view of totality, the concept cause attains a limiting character, the nature of an idea. Therefore, the view of totality, and the idea of origin related to it, belongs to the *limiting-functions* of the whole of reality – the functions of faith. In the function of faith, all ideas receive their contents from revelation, i.e., from the *disclosure* of the very essence of reality, which cannot be disclosed conceptually by theoretical analysis. In other words, this subject is a matter of faith. It is often called dogma or axioma, but this terminology describes the issue less precisely.

Thus, a person's concrete faith in an origin of all existence (the totality) also belongs to the experience of meaning.

The Question of a Destination

The third major element in the question of the meaning of life is the issue of destination. In our colloquial speech the word "meaning" sometimes refers only to the issue of a destination. This usage is usually acceptable because "meaning," as a concept, has taken this as one of its parts. In the philosophical totality-view, this concept is deepened in its meaning to an idea. The idea of meaning, like the idea of origin, is then directed to the converging, perspectival centre, the concentration and synopsis of all ends in one all-embracing total destiny. It is also true that this idea, both as a question and as an idea, arises from the theoretical analysis of the reality of life.

Likewise, we must admit that philosophy itself does not provide the answer to this question of destination. Nor can any other science, not even psychology or theology, furnish us with such an answer. As a question it is answered, and as an idea it acquires its contents from the limiting-function of our existence, i.e., from our faith.

This limiting-function acts like a window in our existence. Through the window, the light from outside and above enters our life and enlightens it. This is the true meaning of the real enlightenment, which escaped the philosophy and theology of the Enlightenment. "The light shines on in the dark and the dark has never mastered it" (John 1:5). The Enlightenment merely substituted the light of reason

251

for the light of revelation.

The Three Central Relations – Anthropological Distinctions

In concrete life, man finds meaning in three central relations. This is generally accepted to be the case, although people may differ on the precise anthropological formulation. In Christian anthropology, Dooyeweerd gave his own typical elaboration on this theme. The intended relations are those between man and God, between man and his fellow-men, and between man and his world. The latter can also be called the "I-self-relation." A closer look at these three will prove helpful.

Dooyeweerd's usual formulation of these "central religious relations" gave rise to some misunderstanding. He calls these relations "central" because man's total concrete existence and experience is related to the "ego" as the transcending and transcendent centre of our life. Man's life evolves from the ego in a diverging direction and is directed again to the ego in a converging direction, in the concentration of all experience on himself. Here I am thinking about the experience of identity, the experience of life as *my* life, and thus also about "self-reflection."

But Dooyeweerd also employs the term "central-religious." He even uses the expression "religious sphere." This could have caused the misunderstanding that religion has a "seat" in the "ego" or heart of man (which can easily be located). But this is not the view

252

of Dooyeweerd, although for the sake of convenience he more than once made use of this traditional terminology. Neither the ego nor the three central-religious relationships in which the ego functions are religious in the sense that our concrete temporary existence would *not* be religious. There is no separate "sphere," distinct from our temporary existence, that *is* religion or would be religious in *nature* or where religion is *seated*. No, the whole of human existence is religious; we stand in relation to God. For this reason, the following succinct formulation is applicable: "man does not *have* religion, man *is* religion."

Our human existence and experience is "virtually" concentrated in one focal point. In the same way, one can say that the all-encompassing religious relationship with God is concentrated "centrally" in the unity of the religious choice or surrender of the heart. The hyphen in "central-religious" indicates that "central" is accentuated and refers to the religious *fullness* of meaning in the centre of life; here the totality of life is concentrated as a unity.

The I-Self-Relation

In psychology this expression has the status of a technical term. It is derived from the way we occa-sionally speak of ourselves reflexively: I can't do this to myself, I control myself, I laugh at myself, I remind myself, I hurt myself, etc. The linguistic technical term "reflexive pronoun" (me, myself) indicates that a certain activity starts out from the subject (the ego) but also returns to this subject. When I hurt myself, *I* suffer pain. If I control myself, I control *something of myself*, e.g., my temper, emotion, language, etc. If I confer with myself, speak to myself, consult myself, these examples indicate that I must distinguish something in my existence which cannot be separated from it and cannot exist apart.

Philosophers have often occupied themselves with this phenomenon. But usually they interpret this acting subject – which always remains the subject itself and can never become its own object – as the subject of thought or subject of the will. This was the result of a view of human existence that reduced human subjectivity to mere volition and thought.

Following Dooyeweerd we want to introduce a distinction in our concrete experience between "ego" and "selfhood" between "I" and "myself" (notice the examples above once again). *All* our subjective functions, not only perception and thought, are aspects of our temporary existence, which we transcend in the centre of our existence – our "ego."

All our many and varied kinds of activities *emanate* from the centre of our "ego," but our "ego" does not in any way stay beyond; it is always there. I speak, I love, I act justly, I think, I look, etc. But I am more than my speech, my love, my acts, my looking, etc. During all the years between birth and death, in spite of all the many drastic changes that "I" undergo, I am still the self-same person. In other words, I transcend my temporary functions in my supra-temporal transcendent ego.

For this reason, my concrete existence is not only an expression of who and what I am, but in its temporary diversity it is again and again focussed on my own identity and is experienced as "of me" or "my own." On this "centre" we focus all our experiences as "our" (own) experiences. We do this in the process of "self-reflection."

A good example here would be the parable of the prodigal son. He took stock of the ruins of his life at the trough of the pigs and considered what a good life he had earlier enjoyed at home with his father. Then he surveyed all that had happened to him since then and where he had landed. In the end, he "came to himself." The result of his communion with himself was his confession: Father, I have sinned against heaven and against you.

The German word "die Sammlung," in the sense of self-contemplation, exactly describes this firm grip on the diversity of life – this convergence of all life's diversity on one denominator. Not only our thought but all our activities are directed to the nucleus of our deepest existence.

Unfortunately, we have no other way to describe this nucleus, this being, this depth, except by way of metaphorical language. It transcends our comprehension and our concepts – we are the self! It is for this reason that Dooyeweerd alternately speaks of ego and selfhood, even though he means one and the same thing. In theoretical anthropology I recommend the consistent use of *"ego"* for the transcendent, "supra-temporal" ego as concentration-point of our whole concrete human existence in time. "Self" could be used to describe this temporary existence.

The Uniqueness of the I-Self-Relation

In light of the previous paragraph, I could offer the following conclusions. There are two realities that stand in a relationship to each other in the I-self-relationship. There is the concrete temporary existence and experience of human life (the self). And there is also the "virtual" centre, the nucleus of the personality. Here existence is centered in a focal point from which all concrete acts emanate. This focal point is also at the centre of the identity experience, i.e., the experience of something as of myself or characteristic of me.

In a sense this "I," as transcendence, lies outside our structured temporary existence in which it is active and manifests itself. This "I" can therefore be compared to the focal point of a magnifying glass which is situated outside the glass but as a focal point still determines the whole form and function of the magnifying glass. It is called a "virtual focal point."

Let us turn to the dynamics in the I-self-relation. These are of two kinds. On the one hand this relation is an *expression*-relation. The I (ego) manifests itself in the self and gives direction to the existence of the self in orientation to the horizon of experience. In this direction the human personality unfolds itself in the vast diversity of experience and in the types of acts and actions.

On the other hand, the I-self-relation is also a relation of *experience*. Here we see the converging or concentrating tendency in life through which we experience all the expressions of our lives as our own. We concentrate these on the meaning of our existence in the process of self-reflection. In this way we "come to ourselves" ("Sammlung").

In both tendencies found in the dynamics of human life, attention must be paid to the correlation between law-side and subject-side. The tendency to divert or unfold is subject to the *law of expression* or the *law of unfolding (developing)*, which is the very source of this dynamic. The tendency to convert or concentrate is subject to control by the *concentration-law*, which compels us to introspection or self-reflection.

Reducing our World of Experience to What is Theoretically Accessible

Our temporary existence is totally interwoven with our world. All kingdoms are integrated in it: the kingdom of minerals, the kingdom of plants, the kingdom of animals as well as humanity. To many people there is more to existence because they are conscious of a still wider horizon of experience. They take into consideration God or the gods, the realm of the dead, angels, and demons. We would create a false reduction and restriction of human experience if we left these out of our consideration.

To a great extent this reduction process was

set in motion by the major role assigned to science during the Enlightenment in European culture. From this perspective the reduction process was to be expected, because the realm of the dead and the evil spirits and benevolent spirits is not accessible theoretically. Scientifically it cannot be analysed because it is accessible to *faith* alone. In the name of Enlightenment, reason forced faith back as far as possible, but faith desperately tried to exert its influence through a sustained effort.

Faith definitely has problems in the sparse idealism of philosophical ego-metaphysics, the abstract and absolutized *idea* of freedom. For this reason, faith has reappeared in full force in: (a) the re-mythologizing of science and politics; (b) the ever-growing interest in parapsychology, para-normal phenomena, spiritualism, etc.; (c) the current introduction of numerous associations for Oriental mysticism. But even here faith has a struggle. Faith became warped and introspective. It is not really "transcendent" but instead a completely "immanent" meditation. It gropes about in the dark caverns of self-estrangement because of alienation from God.

Interlacement of the Self and the Non-Human World

In which way is our "self" interlaced with the non-self of what we call "our world"? If we consider the organic and psychic aspects of our existence, it is clear that in our temporary existence we are subject to the same laws as those designed for minerals and "living nature." The laws of number, space, movement, energy, organic and sensitive life are just as valid for man as for the earthly non-human life. These laws do not only apply to all these things, they make possible all things subjected to these laws. They are the sustaining ground and propelling force. What is more, these laws unite their "subjects" as belonging members of the same "kind." For this reason, there is a close affinity between humans and the non-human world in the six aspects noted above.

Interlacement of the Self and the Fellow-Man (or "the other")

We should also consider the whole interlacement of the societal relationships with all its different types and sub-types. This is why we say that part of the essence of man is to be a fellow-man (or neighbour). Co-humanity in this respect is not an aspect, like, for example, the social or moral aspect. What we have in mind here is *all* aspects and even more, because man in his relationships with other people functions in all aspects, of which the social and moral aspects are only two. Our whole self is interlaced with the self of the neighbour(s) or the other(s). This interlacement is our "world," our temporary way of existence.

Transcending the I-Self-Relation

This temporary way of existence of our fellow-man is an expression of his life-centre. For this reason, the I-self-relation transcends the entire temporary existence of the self and of the other in the I-you-relation. The *I-you*-relation *manifests* itself in the self-other-relation. The self-other-relation is both my world and his world, our world and their world, our individual "worlds" are interlaced with each other in "our world," our temporal way of existence and experience. This point is important for the subsequent epistemological problem. Our knowledge of man has its boundaries in the possibility of experiencing the ways in which my fellow-man *expresses* himself.

The Insufficiency of the Formulation "I-You-Relation"

The second central relation is that with our neighbour, our fellow-man. I deliberately describe the relation in this way because the expression *I-thou-relation*, which has been so popular since the time of Martin Buber, reminds us too much of an encounter between two persons. If we broaden the scope of this term, it becomes clear that we have to make some finer distinctions in this relationship.

In the first place, the two terms "neighbour" and "fellow-man" not only refer to our contemporaries, but also to our ancestors and descendants. Our life is interlaced with our culture, which to a great extent is formed by our ancestors. Similarly, we, in our culture, determine the life of posterity. For this reason, we feel anxious about the problem of energy and environment, we write books, establish organisations, and participate in politics.

In the Dutch language there is a distinction

between "naaste" (neighbour) (the one *near* to you) and "verste" (the one *far* from you). Nicolai Hartmann uses "versteliefde" when he speaks of love and care for posterity – the world of tomorrow in which our descendants must live. There is also another interpretation of "versteliefde," namely to care for our fellow-men who live far away in the Third World. To my mind we can include all of these aspects in the term "humanity," or simply the "human family," of which we ourselves are members.

Temporal Human Existence as an Expression of the Human Person

This thought is significant for the distinction we must make in the I-you-relation. Just as in the case of the I-self-relation, this expression fails to reflect all that is involved. The I-thou-relation to which Martin Buber devoted so much attention is simply not the same as the interlacement of our temporary human existence. The truth is that our interpersonal social relations are the expression of humans as persons. But the person is more than his temporary structural existence, which he in any case transcends in the "I" of his existence. The temporary existence of the other belongs to my world, to myself. Naturally this concerns only a small part of my self, of "My world." All of these concerns depend on the nature and number of societal relations in which I stand.

Because man's temporary existence is his *field of expression* and *possibility of expression*, I come in deeper intuitive contact with the heart of my fellow-men via these fields of expression.

Knowledge of Human Nature

I am not, of course, referring merely to *knowledge*-contact. We can touch the heart of someone by way of other functions, or acts other than mental acts. Certain specific deeds can sometimes establish a deeper contact than mental contact or word-contact. But knowledge-contact is possible and belongs to our realm of contact.

As practical, intuitive, or theoretical knowledge of our fellow-men, this knowledge of human nature has a transcending relationship (or alignment) to the heart of the other. No direct knowledge of the heart of our fellow-men is possible. Anthroposophic mysticism pursues this object in vain. What we know of our fellow-men, we know only via their self-manifestation in the concrete practice of their lives. This we know directly, via others, or by other means.

The knowledge we thus gain of the other can only be formulated in categories of time, i.e., concepts and judgements that have a bearing on the functioning of our fellow-men in the structured relation of our existence in time. But the converging and transcending *alignment* of one heart to another is intrinsic to this knowledge of human nature.

The more this knowledge of human nature penetrates (via these external expressions of life) to the deeper dimensions of our human functioning, the "deeper" we call our knowledge of men. But in the end, we arrive in the border-area, the bottom layer, the *ethos*. In other words, when we approach the depth of the human heart, we approach the limits of our knowledge of men. However, this approach must never be confused with "depth psychology"!

The Ethos as Border-Area of our Knowledge

We will presently see that it is quite difficult to know this border-area or ethos. But some knowledge of it is still possible because this border-area belongs to the field of expression of the human person. What we can thereby conclude of the "condition" of the human heart as religious concentration point can only take the form of a judgement, because: (a) this is a judgement of faith; (b) this is in no way a result of theoretical analysis (and consequently no result of psychology); and (c) this is a human, fallible and preliminary judgement, because the contents of this judgement transcend human knowledge and are only open completely to the eyes of God.

The Bible says that God sees the *heart*.

By way of analogy, we can say that our knowledge of human nature allows us to make a distinction between a person's deeds and his *attitude* or *ethos*. But we must be conscious of the fact that knowledge of the ethos is not the final word about it and never will be. Behind the ethos, the transcending secret of the human person is hidden, a secret only known to God.

The Transcending Moment in the "I-You-Relation"

We say that, together with our fellow-men, we transcend our mutual structural existence in our supra-structural "I." This, too, is no purely individual affair. Individuals – in a radical sense – do not exist, neither in their mutual interlacement with the whole of our temporary world, nor in their transcendent hearts. What we know and can state about these matters is derived exclusively from the Bible; only faith pronouncements are possible. Philosophy as well as theology should remain silent on this subject. The expression "the family of man" is only a clever metaphor for the totality of humanity.

The Unique Spiritual community of Mankind

From biblical revelation we know that there exists a transcendent, central-religious community between people on the deepest level of their existence. Moreover, humanity can be reduced in this religious community to one denominator – namely "man" (Hebrew: adam). In this respect, humanity differs from the animal kingdom. In theology this quality is analogically called the "corporative character" of humanity. As soon as we forget the anthropo*logical* and ana*logical* character of this term and convert it into a social *category*, then any possible conception is already excluded. Man is not a social structure in a temporary sense, but the supra temporal, supra-structural, "spiritual" unity of humanity.

This unity is not a product of abstract thought, nor a concept or idea, but a reality comprehensible only to faith. The Bible refers to this unity by different names, including "the body of Christ." This spiritual community of mankind first became real in one *person*, the first man: Adam. After the fall, this central representative function of the head of humanity passed on to Christ, the "second Adam," at least for those who are "incorporated" in Christ by the Holy Spirit through faith.

For this reason, the transcendent depth-dimension of the I-you-relation is seated in the spiritual community of the "body of Christ," of which Christ Himself is the representative and substitute head (Rom. 12, 1 Cor. 12). Here we see the meaning of the unique biblical expression "to be in Christ." This community only has an analogy in the temporary structures of social relationships between people. It can be compared to but not identified with the unity and complexity of an organism, a "body."

The Relation between God and Humanity

Neither of the two relations we discussed – the I-self-relation and the I-you-relation – exists by itself. The most essential, primary characteristic of the world and humanity is that they stand in a relation to God, their origin. This is the relation of creation. The relation to the origin is at the same time the relation to the destination. It is true of the whole cosmos and man that God is the Source, Guide and Goal of all that is (Rom. 11:36). This is why the three central relations do not stand next to each other on the same level. The relation to God founds and includes both the others. This foundational relation is not a variant or equivalent of the I-you-relation within humanity.

The Image-Relation between God and Man

We believe that man was created in the image of God, and this has a special meaning for us. It is a revealed truth with very comprehensive contents and far-reaching implications. By implication, man is nothing in himself because he is a reflection of God and has the *source* of his whole existence and way of existence in God. (The doctrine of man as the image of God plays a major role in theology.)

In addition, man in all his relations has the gift and the calling to be "like God" (in a human way); man must be equal to God not in autonomy but in an orientation to God's creational will. To acquire knowledge of God's will and to act accordingly should fill his life. That this hardly ever happens, according to the Bible, is a result of the "total corruption" of humanity because of sin and God's judgement on sin. However, the theological discussion of sin is not a theme of philosophy, not even of philosophical ethology ("ethics") or of the philosophy of history.

Conclusion: The Question of Meaning

Being conscious of the meaning of existence while living in the three central-religious relations, man finds the answers to the major questions of life. The meaning issue leads to the questions of origin, way of existence and destination, and these questions require an answer which has a religious character or stems from faith.

Fall, Alienation and Self-Alienation

There is a direct connection between the fall and alienation from God, and the fundamental (concerning the deepest intention of life) estrangement between man and fellow-man. The problems caused by the fall and alienation in the three central human relationships are experienced unhappily. Viewed from the law-side, man is constantly called, commanded, invited, and even tempted to aspire to *happiness*. Happiness requires an end to alienation by way of reconciliation with God, our neighbour, and our self, resulting in intense Peace.

Types of Ethos and the Answer to the Meaning-Question

In response to this call to be truly human, man offers many answers. When the only true answer is not given to God in faith and love, man finds in the non-divine, in creation, many possibilities to create or project *substitutes for God.* Herein lies the exact point of contact for the classification of the ethos-types. Here we see the fundamental mental attitudes that humanity adopts in respect to the central questions of life which we confront in our "view of life."

267

Problems with Classification and the "History of Mentality"

The point of contact for the classification of the ethos in history is to a great extent still quite formal. Even those who do not practise their philosophy from a certain Christian viewpoint could take it over. Still, non-adherents will not likely pose the problem in the same way.

Sometimes when the question of meaning or of origin and destination is approached by means of the central question about the way of existence, an imprecise or general answer is offered. Inevitably, this leads to statements that cannot be founded intelligibly on evidence nor even less on logical argumentation. Here we land in the border-area of science where philosophy (i.e., anthropology and praxiology) poses the deepest, first and last questions – without being able to give an answer. The answer does not originate in human *thought*; it comes from outside and is understood and received by man through his *faith-function*.

When we then say that these answers are answers of faith, we are correct. But we must take into consideration that no single faith is pure subjective phantasy; every faith is always a more or less positive or negative answer to the *self-revelation of the Origin*. The influence of this self-revelation can be known in all existence, but specially and centrally in the Holy Scriptures. This is the intention of theology when it offers the less fortunate formulation of "general and special revelation," i.e., revelation in created reality and the Holy Scripture.

Although we are conscious of how we depart from the current practices with our historical method, we still think we are compelled to use it in view of our survey of the reality of the ethos itself. In spite of different aprioristic rejections of this method, it still has an advantage: we can expect greater clarity in our investigation of the history of the ethos than from the confusing, ever more hesitant, and more sceptical current methods.

Huizinga struggled with the problem of putting into words the so-called *spirit* of the Renaissance, but he was unsuccessful. However, we can now see some progress in that there is a growing demand for a "mentality-history." But if we take notice of the efforts, it is clear that the central questions are being posed anew; what really is mentality, and what characteristics are typical for a certain mentality?

But then we realise that no history can ever be practised satisfactorily without a systematic background. For this reason, I formerly started studying systematically the anthropological structure and place of the ethos. Only then can a person make any progress in an historical investigation. Then, sometimes unexpectedly, such an investigation may contribute to a clarification of systematic philosophy, wisdom, and knowledge not only of "spiritual affairs in the religious sector," but also of the common everyday things which comprise our responsibilities. In this context, therefore, it is good to remind ourselves and one another that the Bible often speaks about the prayer for the Holy Ghost, while "supplication" is often added to the ordinary "prayer."

Scientific and Structural Theory

Yet this prayer for the indispensable guidance of the Spirit of Christ is no less important than our responsibility and activity. On the contrary, this prayer is the most important part of it. Prayer, however, is not the only thing in life. In prayer we respond only to *one* Word of God. But God's creative and redeeming Word constitutes our *whole* life and *every* situation. Therefore, every situation comes to us with an appeal, a "challenge," to which we must answer. Previously we saw that our human responsibility is the directedness of our life to the creation-and redemption-Word.

In the whole complex of our total response to God our Creator and Redeemer, the law to distinguish well with our *reason* plays an important part. This law is so important that when He formulates the great commandment of love, Christ declares that we must love the Lord our God "with our whole mind."

In our responsibility to make "good use of our mind," scientific reflection plays an important role. It has a special direct responsibility in scientific work, and in the application of the results of scientific work in our practical lives.

CHAPTER 13

Responsibility

Introduction: Popular Words

EVERY PERIOD HAS its own operative words. Today we cannot reason without terms like responsibility, humanitarianism, democratising, progressiveness, values, etc. Whoever wishes to discuss social issues, for example, will use these words abundantly. As common terms, they strike a certain note; they seem to echo a particular attitude toward life.

The great popularity of such words does not depend on their conceptual clarity, but in their extraordinary *resonance* in a certain mentality or sphere. It does not matter at all that certain words might have various meanings, as does the word "democracy," for example. In its own milieu, such as the Western World or the Eastern block, the meaning is understood, although it may be quite the opposite of what is meant elsewhere by the same term.

I do not think it wise to be disparaging about such terms, despite their multiple meanings, ambiguity, popularity, or misuse. It is better to ask oneself how a certain word has become so popular. What is the resonance in such a word? What touches modern man so fundamentally in such a word that when he hears it, he is prepared to listen to the speaker? Conversely, why is communication restricted and even cut off by the use of certain words?

In this chapter we should like to discuss the current popularity of the term "responsibility." This discussion will be based mainly on the philosophy of the Cosmonomic Idea.

Response/Answer

It will be worthwhile to start our discussion by looking at the literal content of the concept "responsibility." Such an approach is not always fruitful, but for our Christian view of human responsibility I find it necessary. "Responsibility" is derived from "respond" (Latin-spondere). "Re" means again in return; "spondere" means promise.

The meaning of "answerable" derives from a word and a reaction to a word. Response/answer in its most general meaning is a reaction to a word; it is a response to a promise.

Now, if we consider that responsibility is related to being human (includes human actions), then a few simple questions cannot be avoided. Who is the speaker of the word? Who gives the answer? What is this word and what is this answer all about? In other words, what is the content of both? Something can still be said about the terms we can deduce from

272

these central concepts promise/word and response/ answer namely responsibility, co-responsibility, accountability. If we succeed in answering these questions in the light of the Scriptures, we may be better equipped to bear our many responsibilities in practical life.

Philosophical Orientation

The philosophy of the Cosmonomic Idea has pursued philosophy in the light of the Scriptures and can rejoice in some preliminary results. It has a starting point and a theory of the structure of temporal reality which is governed by the Scriptures. Both of these elements fulfil their role in scientific thought by supplying an initial orientation. The Christian view of life, which is not scientific in character, is thereby deepened and enriched. This initial orientation will suffice for the theme of this chapter.

The above-mentioned starting point is the Cosmonomic Idea or the "transcendental ground-idea." Dooyeweerd preferred the latter term to the older term Cosmonomic Idea. In the philosophy of the Cosmonomic Idea (as in other philosophical trends), this ground-idea is three-dimensional and refers to the coherence, unity, and origin of wholeness in the abundant variety of life.

In colloquial language, just as in any specific science, many words and fundamental concepts can be discussed in the light of this three-dimensional ground-idea. These words are then clarified and become more useful. This point will be illustrated as

273

we look at the concept "responsibility."

Origin of Responsibility: Word and Response

In the biblical accounts of creation, we learn that God created man after His own image and likeness. We note how God spoke to man and gave him instructions. God entered into a covenant for life with Abraham and his descendants. As a result, we begin to see how the promise understood in the concept "responsibility" is to be sought primarily in the creative Word of God. The response is then the response of man to God's Word and promises.

If the mutual relationship between God and man was only a part of human existence, only a religious sector that existed alongside the rest of life, then it would be of little value to dwell on this religious outlook. One could just as well reflect on the many different responsibilities of man in everyday life "irrespective of God." But then some simple fundamental questions (to whom and to what man responds) require a totally different answer.

F. Heineman states clearly that instead of offering the Cartesian ground-idea (I think, therefore I am), one must say: "I answer, therefore I am." He describes man as a responsive being and elaborates on this premise in an initially fascinating theory. Soon, however, it becomes clear that this process of answering/responding is really an answer to various stimuli and questions of a physical, biotic, psychic, and socio-cultural nature. He does not inquire any further into the origin of these stimuli and questions. The *origin* of our responsiveness does not, in his opinion, lie in the Word of God. Therefore, as far as social relations are concerned, his conclusion dwells on a personalistic conception of responsibility. We shall return to this problem in a moment.

In the Christian view of life, however, the confession of God as creator and origin of human life is emphasised: the creation-word that rang out called life into existence. The Scriptures say God is the Source, Guide, and Goal of all that is (Rom. 11:36; cf. 1 Cor. 8:6). Being the "goal" of all life does not concern only the eschatological salvation of man but also his whole concrete existence here and now. Every facet, every sector of his life, is created out of God, through God and for God. All life has an inner structural directedness to God.

The Creation-Word

Readers of the Bible know that we are not engaged in mere word-play when we seek the divine origin of human responsibility in the creation-word of God. The gospel states clearly in John 1 that everything has been created by the Word Of God. Even if it is clear that by using "Word of God" John meant the Son of God, it is still worth noting that God's Son is called "The Word." In Christ the Trinity expresses Himself, reveals Himself, His love, His will, His thoughts, His power.

275

Repeatedly we find the same thought in connection with the creation in the Bible. Psalm 33:6 says: "By the word of the Lord were the heavens made; and all the host of them by the breath of his mouth." And Hebrews 11:3 testifies: "Through faith we understand that the worlds were framed by the word of God . . ." The unfathomable quality of this divine creation through the Word is enlarged again by a remark of St. Paul in Romans 4:17. Although he does not deal directly with creation, he dwells on the omnipotence that God shows in His redeeming word. To express this quality, Paul uses creation terminology: in the redeeming word (re-creation!) we stand before the work of this God who not only "gives life to the dead," but who also "calls into being that which does not exist." In both re-creation and creation, God's words are *active* words.

Human Life Is a Response

If we want to express ourselves philosophically, we can state that the existence of man was *called into being* by the creation-word of God. Therefore, life is always concerned with the creation-word of God, who maintains this creation-word. This life-creating, calling-into-being Word of God demands a certain way of living in which man should express his voluntary and mutual love for God. Consequently, the creative word of God *makes* man responsible (answerable). Man answers God with his life, simply by living.

The nature of the answer is not very important. What matters is that this life is still an answer, a response, a re-action to God's creative action, offered through the power of the creative act. No concrete human responsibility can be either primarily or exclusively a responsibility towards one's fellowman or a particular situation. The origin of human life stands in a relation to God as Creator, and this fact can never be ignored or repealed. Human life, when lived according to creation, is always and primarily a response to God.

God's Presence in Life

In Christ, God still reveals his once spoken creation-word and He enforces its powerfully. After all, God did not cast man into the world after creation as a finished product and leave him to himself. On the contrary, God's Word remains the sustaining power of man and the world. When it is said of Christ that in Him all things were created (Col. 1:16), the other word that Hebrews 1:2-3 mentions is already implied: "through whom (Christ) also He made the world" (everything that was, is and will be). And He is the radiance of His glory and the exact representation of His nature, and *upholds all things by the word of His power . . .*"

This all-sustaining, powerful Word of God-in-Christ is the divine mystery of life. In a biblical sense it is "God's presence" in life. It is His ever-actual, working presence-in-the-Word, the creative Word and recreative Word that is and remains the same Word. To this Word, human life is a re-sponse and answer. Thus, there is no contradiction or tension

277

between the creative Word and the redeeming Word. In Christ they are one because Christ Himself is the Word of God.

The endless tension and contradictions lie in man's answer to the creation. He is a responsive being and has an answer-structure. As a result, the evil that occurs on the side of man can never be judged neutrally, because it is a negative answer to the positive, creative, and redeeming Word of God. This is also the cause of and reason for the existence of evil in the community. Without God's permanent presence with his active Word-in-life, enforcing will, judgement, and grace, everything that exists turns into nothingness.

No "Creatio Continua" or "Neuschöpfung"

The lasting and active presence of God in life should not be understood in the theological sense of continuous creation ("creatio continua"). This idea draws God's creation-work into time; the biblical revelation of God's faithfulness is lost in God's bondage and subjection to his own works and what man has made of them.

This twisted conception has now created some unfortunate problems. The development of a "theology of revolution," for example, has been a direct result. God is now "employed" (creatio continua) in the current socio-structural changes, particularly when these go in a direction which can

278

be appreciated from a biblical point of view.

The well-known evil of identification (God's case and our case) now returns in a new shape. In this view of life, man is the creator and re-creator of the historically determined community. The Christian faith then "blesses" a revolution (including the weapons) with a theological sanction. God makes all things "new" through people who improve their social structures.

Meanwhile the real presence of God is ignored. The lasting creative and recreative word of God, revealed in Christ and in the order of creation which point to Him, is not heard anymore. The biblical thought of the restoration of creation through Christ is not understood as re-creation but as "Neuschöpfung," a totally different creation, later, after the *creatio continua*, or in dialectical contradiction during the *creatio continua*. Human responsibility is severed from the creative and redeeming Word and is personally misinterpreted in a sort of docetic faith relation. God's creative Word disappears from the redeeming Word.

Man, a Responsive Being

We have already mentioned Heineman's belief that man is a responsive being, a thought which often occurs in anthropological literature. The credibility of this view depends on man's idea about which word he will respond to and to whom this answer will be given. We saw that Heineman refers to various "stimuli" from the nature of man (physical, biotic, socio-culturally, etc.), which urge and challenge him to offer a response or answer. What is omitted in this view is God and His presence in, and in relation to, nature (including history). This makes Heineman's vision of man's responsive being and of human responsibility wholly unacceptable.

The Christian anthropologies teach us that whoever sees man "irrespective of God" strongly misrepresents both human reality and social reality. We must never forget this warning.

Although human responsibility, as a result of its consistently valid relation to the origin, is always and primarily response-to-God, the last word on the subject has been spoken. We must still reflect on the response that man must give to the challenge of his situation or to fellow human-beings in various relations. Needless to say, this is not a new subject but merely different dimensions of the same subject.

The deepest and most fundamental relation to God the origin creates and constitutes the whole responsive being of man. The concrete human responsibilities in the community, even if they seem far removed from faith and religion, are in reality nowhere and never severed from the realm of creation, the all-encompassing life-answer which man gives to God. This answer-structure of man, created by God, gives a beginning, stimulus, and direction to human responsibility in concrete life.

This thought will be expounded more closely in a moment. After looking closely at the origin, we must examine the unity of our responsibilities in the light of the Scriptures.

Christ: The Answer, Our Answer

In the confusing diversity of life with its various responsibilities, man is seeking a pattern, a line, a style, a perspective. When he reflects on his life and (like the prodigal son) "comes to himself," he often unconsciously seeks to reduce the innumerable factors of his life to *one* denominator.

Luckily the Bible indicates a very clear way. In the person, the work, and the Word (i.e., in the kingdom of Christ the denominator), the perspectival centre of our life is revealed by God. An almost excessive amount of words and thoughts in the Holy Scriptures directs our life to that focal-point in which all our responsibilities are concentrated and where we find ourselves.

It is therefore almost impossible to concentrate the deeper unity of our responsibility in one term or expression. In actual faith we can express it simply by one word, namely Christ, in whom we have our life through the communion of the Holy Ghost. "Jesus, life of our life."

Missing Unity: Moralism

We can lose our way in the great variety of our responsibilities in life if we look for a pattern, line, or perspective. We are bewildered because we fancy the centre, the unity, or the perspective of our respon-

281

sibilities to be in the wrong place and we therefore experience it inaccurately. The precise responsibility that takes hold of us existentially starts to function as our perspectival unity and centre. Thus we see one specific responsibility or complex of responsibilities as central, and we allow it to govern our lives.

It is typical of secularised Christianity to let a few moral responsibilities fulfil this central role. From the viewpoint of a supposedly inviolable evidence, such an attitude is "identified" with an "evangelical" attitude. Preferably, one then speaks of an "evangelical inspiration." This term replaces the older "Christian aims" of Roman Catholics and "Christian principles" of Protestants.

In most cases the contents of this "evangelical inspiration" seems to fall in line with liberal-humanistic Christianity. Christ is seen as the highest revelation and realisation of neighbourly love, forming the centre of a humanistic view of life and thereby absolutized. Because of the romantic flavour of the words "neighbourly love" (humanity), the term "humanitarianism" has become the keyword for the propaganda of liberal-humanistic Christianity.

Humanitarianism

The term "humanitarianism" does not simply refer to the fact that all people are one another's neighbours. This word has obtained a strong and almost exclusively *moral* sense in modern usage. It also has a clear and strong normative function. People ask consistently for the humanising or moralising of *all* human relations and societal structures, which shows that the absolutizing of humanitarianism (in the moral sense) is already far advanced. The same is true of politics, business life, ecclesiastic community, judicature, etc.

This phenomenon shows an apparent deficiency. Despite the presence of Christianity, neighbourly love (humanity) in Western culture has fallen short to such an extent that it now re-asserts its repressed rights. In more general terms, the historical development of science, technique, and organisation has forced man into a predicament. In this context Shelsky refers to the modern "myth of man." He says this myth functions in reality, but it is not clear what "man" is or ought to be.

Human freedom in particular is more threatened than ever before, and mankind tries to save this freedom by way of the "mystical" call for "humanity" and "humanitarianism." Often the norm of humanitarianism (in a moral sense) is subservient to this "humanity:" neighbourly love primarily honours the *freedom* of the neighbour. In the end, human responsibility *serves* personal freedom and the freedom of others. Unfortunately, many people forget that this freedom is fundamentally an inverted (perverted) Christian freedom, which can be clearly seen in the personalistic handling of the concepts "humanity" and "responsibility."

The moralistic absolutizing of the "ethics" of neighbourly love in human relations can be appreciated as an historical correction of other absolutizations

283

in society. Unfortunately, this absolutizing is of a reactionary nature and hence misses the point of real progression. Already contra-revolutionary ideas are circulating in a new reaction which is being called forth by this one-sidedness.

Although this current absolutizing of moral neighbourly love is a reaction to the deficiency of neighbourly love in Western culture, the Gospel does not advocate this reactionary way. The only genuine and true progression orients itself in the direction that God as Creator and Redeemer gives to human life in the human response-structure. God outlined for us the beginning and direction of our lives in dotted lines and chalk stripes. In our lives we have to walk along these dotted lines. As the image of God, and on the basis of the divine *principles* of creation, we may proceed as his fellow-workers. We are to give norms and forms to life even in the continuous renewal of the *subjective*, organisational "structures of society" formed in history.

In Search of Unity: The Harmonious Balance

Those who seek a theoretical balance also demand our attention. They warn modern man that in his reaction to our "technical culture" he should not, in the name of humanitarianism, fall victim to a certain cultural pessimism; he should not look at "objective" culture disparagingly. According to these balance-seekers, human responsibility must be operative in the centre of political and economic power-relations, without rancour toward power. Humanity must be treated according to its merit, i.e., in the *centre* of the development of science, political power structures and organisational structures. *Harmony* is its central point. The powers of organisational structures, politicians, religious groupings and even of armies must attain harmonious balance and become serviceable to "humanity."

Even so, the central norm and unity of our various responsibilities, seen in the light of our Christian view of life, does not lie in a balanced cultural development. Doubtless this balance is worth pursuing. In every concrete responsibility a certain element of balance must be recognised and respected. It is possible, however, that one can fail in real responsibility because of one-sidedness or a limited outlook.

If the element of balance in our responsibilities should represent the highest wisdom, we are taking a very weak stand indeed. The conflicting powers of progression and reaction usually take very little notice of this fine balance. Moreover the "harmoniously developed man" (a dated humanistic ideal) is called "the most boring creature that exists." This description could be applied to culture and society. *Real* harmony is not oriented to the balance between rival powers of culture, each absolutizing a different aspect of the human answer-structure.

No matter how important the element of balance is, true harmony does not only seek balance; it also

285

seeks a *centre*, a perspective, an inspiring denominator. Only by encouraging all aspects of human responsibility to aim for this denominator will true balance emerge.

True balance is not dependent on accidental, temporary, or periodically returning culture-dominants – the rival absolutizations. The intended balance orients itself to the perspective of the kingdom of God. Without this perspective, every search for cultural balance by humanists will follow a road leading nowhere. Because of man's created answer-structure, he keeps looking for the centre and unity of all responsibilities.

The Real Unity: Love

In the kingdom of Christ, all human responsibilities receive their consolidation and unity of direction in complete service to God. From Cod and to God all things are ("ta panta"). Man and world stand in the perspective of Christ and his kingdom. Christ Himself sought and found the unity of His (our) answer to life in the light of the Scriptures. He formulated the unity of God's creation-word (the law, thora) and of the human answer evoked by it in the dual commandment of love. "On these two commandments depend the whole law and the prophets," including the proclamation of the creation. The phrase "the whole law and the prophets" implies that in the great commandment of love all *performing Words* of God in creation and redemption are united. This *one* central command is not merely one paragraph of law among

286

many others. It is spirit and life (John 6:63); it is power and wisdom. This command brings healing and salvation from the start and for ever.

Because of this commanding-Word, which is both a Word of creation and a Word of redemption, our life in its unity and totality receives its controlling religious direction. This love is also incarnated in Christ Himself. Love is the central unity of the law of life, i.e., the central unity of the human answer-structure and of the answer to life itself.

As such, love must be distinguished from its moral aspect in social relations. This dual meaning implies terminological problems, but these are not insurmountable.

Scientific Embarrassments

Both theology and philosophy arrive at the frontiers of their scientific possibilities in one respect. They only have inadequate concepts to describe the subjective unity which stands in correlation to the commandment of love. Followers of the philosophy of the Cosmonomic Idea also have terminological problems with this point. Supporters of Dooyeweerd speak of "the supra-temporal concentration point" of the "Archimedean point." Others prefer to speak with Vollenhoven of the "prefunctional heart" of man. Yet others replace the word "supratemporal" with "more-than-temporal," or they restrict themselves to the philosophical technical term "transcendence."

All these terms have their advantages and

disadvantages. A term in itself, however, is not important. We *can* state that the whole philosophy of the Cosmonomic Idea stands or falls with the *insight* expressed in this wavering and deficient way. This insight is not the privilege of the educated.

Insight and Wisdom in Christ

One insight is at the centre of the Christian view of life. It concerns the Christian vision of man and of the community in which the unity of creation and redemption is confessed and formulated. With his heart and life, man answers to the creative and redeeming Word that was and is still being spoken by God in Christ and in the order of creation. Therefore, the individual subjective *unity* of all human responsibility has no substance in itself. Without Christ, neither creation nor recreation exists.

In his heart and life, each individual is placed by God in creation and redemption under the saving commandment of love. Each person is called to participate in and incorporate the spiritual unity of the human race in (Adam) Christ through the Holy Ghost. All life, and thus all responsibility, is integrated and concentrated in Christ.

Herman Ridderbos in his exegesis of the statement of Paul in Col. 1:17 ("in Him all things hold together") says: "Outside Christ every creature and power is disintegrated." The same author, in his excellent book on the doctrine of Paul, writes about the central meaning of Christ in and for the creation:

"Both in virtue of the creation and in virtue of the restoration of the lost coherence of all things in him (Christ), he forms the great point of integration for all that is in heaven and on earth."

The *unity* in all our diverse responsibilities, centred in our heart, exists in the fact that all the life-answers we display in our various "roles" are given religious direction to God. In the personal surrender of our hearts to Him, all our responsibilities in society are placed in the perspective of the meaning of our lives: out of God, through God, and for God. Standing in this perspective, we believe what Paul says in the conclusion of 1 Cor. 1: Christ is given to us as *wisdom* and *righteousness* in our daily practical life.

The Question of Concreteness

Ridderbos' comment is worth repeating: "Outside Christ every creature and power is disintegrated." For our practical life, and thus for the practice of the social sciences as well, it is extremely important to adhere to this integration and concentration of all life in Christ. Similarly, we must not close our eyes to the disintegration of life outside Christ, even if this dis-integration is not always "empirically" perceptible. In fact, what man thinks he perceives empirically in this respect depends totally on his vision of the norms for life.

Our task is not always easy. At first sight, the many responsibilities in daily life seem far removed from the religious unity of our lives. Many Christians justly ask: what should we do about practical life?

What does it mean to live through Christ in concrete terms, here and now? What does life in Christ mean in my profession, in technology, commerce, science, etc.? What does it mean in politics, business life, education, and sports?

The Wisdom of Life through the Holy Ghost

Actually, the "unity" we discussed previously is a unity *in* variety. The insurveyable wealth of human life, with its countless sectors and facets, easily leads us astray when we take decisions purely incidentally – as if that were possible! But it is impossible. In the structure of human existence, there is a deeper "layer" that gives a certain continuity to our actions, even in the most different situations.

This deeper continuity is designated by various words, such as mentality, attitude, morale, ethos, reason, etc. Concerning reason, the philosophers of the Enlightenment were formally correct when they said the highest aim for our lives should be to enlighten our reason. Paul also says something similar in Romans 12:2: "be transformed by the renewing of your mind that you may prove what the will of God is, that which is good and acceptable and perfect." Paul does not expect this renewal of reason to come from more and better objective information, but from the guidance of God's Spirit. What the Old Testament calls "the fear of the Lord," is still the beginning of wisdom. This wisdom outweighs every single piece of "objective information."

In Christian faith, the first and greatest need for the fulfilment of our responsibilities is the presence of the Holy Ghost. According to the Scriptures, the Spirit is the Spirit of wisdom and knowledge, not only of "spiritual affairs in the religious sector," but also of the common everyday things that compose our responsibilities. In this context, therefore, it is good to remind ourselves and one another that the Bible often speaks about the prayer for the Holy Ghost, while "supplication" is often added to the ordinary "prayer."

Scientific Aid and Structural Theory

Meanwhile this prayer for the indispensable guidance of the Spirit of Christ is not less important than our responsibility and activity. On the contrary, this prayer is the most important *part* of it. Prayer however is not the only thing in life. In prayer we re-spond only to *one* word of God. But God's creative and redeeming word constitutes our *whole* life and *every* situation. Therefore, every situation comes to us with an appeal, a "challenge," to which we must answer. Previously we saw that our human responsibility is the directedness of our life to the creation- and redemption- word.

In the whole complex of the response with our whole life to God our Creator and Redeemer, the law to distinguish well with our *reason*, plays an important part. It is so important that when He formulates the great commandment of Love, Christ declares that we must love the Lord our God "with our whole mind."

291

In this responsibility of "the good use of our mind," scientific reflection plays an important role – both in the case of having a special direct responsibility in this type of work, and in the elaboration of the results of scientific work in our practical decisions. Therefore, man attaches great value to scientific intercommunication and consultation in different sectors of life: in the life of faith (Bible-sciences), in business life (economy and sociology), in family life (pedagogy), etc.

From our examples here it is clear that Christians must remain aware of the relativity of this role of science. They cannot expect renewal of life or any well-being from the development of science in the spirit of the "Enlightenment." They know that science does not have the last word in its own domain; even science is "led" by a deeper layer in human existence.

One of the most important preliminary results of studies in the philosophy of the Cosmonomic Idea was that it became aware of how the history of scientific thought *in all faculties* contains many rash examples of the "disintegration" of any scientific thought dissociated from Christ. A conformed closing of eyes and heart would have been easier, but that would have been unfaithful. Adherents of the Cosmonomic Idea cannot and will not denounce this Christian breakthrough in science. However, the programmes, experiments and hypotheses are still in their initial stage of development.

Theory of Structure and Order of Creation

Even in a partly conscious view of life, everyone has a certain orientation. Man is directed to where the light dawns over all the diverse "challenges" with which he is confronted. Most views of life have a rather simple compass. As far as human society is concerned, man orients himself to a few steady points, from which emerges a simple frame of reference, e.g., state and church, labour and sexuality, nature and culture. Within this framework, certain valuable, simple, and "operable" viewpoints develop. In the Christian circle before the war, man knew the triad of church, state, and society, for example.

The deepening, refining, widening, and enriching brought about by the philosophy of the Cosmonomic Idea are to a great extent due to its *structural theory*. Both the theory of the modalities and the theory of individuality structures based on it have broadened our view immensely. This idea is indispensable for an orientation of human responsibilities. Here we must depend directly on the threefold ground-idea, which gives the structural theory its religiously determined contents and direction. For the structural theory, the philosophy of the Cosmonomic Idea is "grafted" onto the biblical thought of the creational order. Nevertheless, this theory has no guarantee of infallibility or scientific correctness. But it does become "partaker with them of the rich root of the olive tree" – partaker of the integration not just in "Israel" but in Christ.

293

In practical life all wisdom and knowledge intuitively depend on the order of creation (singular) and on the more concrete ordinances of creation based on it. Our life is a subjective relation to this mainly *normative* order of creation. Human responsibility is found in our *dependence* on this order in which God reveals His will to create and redeem. Concrete life is thus an answer to the creative and redeeming Word of God. The role of philosophy and the special sciences is to illuminate the structures of these realms and the situations of life. In turn, our practical knowledge is deepened and interwoven in the fulfilment of our responsibilities.

Order of Creation and Metaphysics

Unfortunately, in most theological traditions the idea of the order of creation is strongly influenced by metaphysical thought. Such thinking stems, in turn, from pre-Christian, heathen thought, naturally adapted to biblical thought in scholastic terms. Now that the trend in dogmatic theology and in scientific exegesis is anti-metaphysical, the premise of an order of creation is not at all popular. Memories of conservative practices, the phenomenon of the "German Christian," national socialism and race-discrimination all re-surface.

But we dare not throw out "the baby with the bathwater." The order of creation is thoroughly biblical and of fundamental importance to our responsibility in society. Faced with seemingly endless misconceptions, nothing is left to us but to expose patiently and sharply the simple notion of faith implied in this order.

In this philosophy of the Cosmonomic Idea, the notion of faith is present in the already mentioned threefold ground-idea. The order of creation as the structural order of all temporal existence gives the idea of *coherence* in the great diversity of life. This coherence finds its unity and concentration of perspective in the great commandment of the service of God with our whole heart – the commandment of love. Dissociated from this commandment, or absolutized in practice, the idea of the order of creation immediately becomes pitiful metaphysics.

Surely the most apostatic character of all ancient and modern metaphysics is that it pretends to be able to dissociate itself from the reality (scientifically in any case) of its real origin and unity. Metaphysics is, in essence, a doctrine about being-in-itself, a doctrine concerning "pure facts" and "objective data." From a religious point of view, it does not make much difference which form of metaphysics one adheres to – one that does or does not fancy a rational or voluntary "being" above, behind, or in the "phenomena." Even by negating such a "being," metaphysics receives its inspiration from the same ground-idea and posits an independent existence of things "on-their-own." This is a form of secularism: disintegration dissociated from Christ.

The idea of a neutral science and a neutral, matter-of-fact politics is based on this premise, as is the idea of unprejudiced Bible exegesis. Similarly, most varieties of the theological doctrine of two domains, of humanitarianism, and of Christian humanism have the same basis. From this premise also stems the idea of "the responsible society," in so far as this is represented in ecumenical theology by the idea of solidarity between church and world, and vice versa. Current thought is much less anti-metaphysical than we would like to believe. It is also less concrete and more mythological.

Order of Creation and Science

In the different theories of structure, the various sciences discover the *normative structure* of the way we give our answer to the revealed Creator's will. Philosophy has a task in the most general structures, philosophies of the special sciences tackle the concrete world, and the special sciences come nearest to practical life. Together they provide us with an orientation, a survey of the totality and coherence of our responsibilities.

An interdependence of the sciences also exists in a horizontal as well as a vertical sense. I would like to remind the reader in this context of a German professor in social ethics who starts his lectures every year with this sentence: "Tell me what your anthropology is and I will tell you what view of society you have" (Oswald von Nell Breuning). We agree with this statement. As a result, we have spoken of human life in the light of the threefold ground-idea of origin, unity, and coherence in the diversity of all existence.

Responsible Society

Here it might be worth looking at the well-known definition given by the World Council of Churches: "In a responsible community reigns the freedom of people, people who know that they are responsible for justice and public order and that those who possess political authority or economic power, are responsible to God and to the people whose well-being depend on this."

In the light of our idea of Christian responsibility, a person can criticize this statement to such an extent that very little or nothing is left of it. It is possible to penetrate into this Christian conception. The context in which we find the above quotation gives an even more restricted vision of the responsible society. Yet these words have the benefit of explaining what Mannheim calls "the fundamental democratising of our society."

In order not to elaborate unnecessarily, we restrict ourselves here to a discussion of the important concepts "co-authority" and "co-responsibility."

Fundamental Democracy

The term "democracy" has, in the past few centuries, acquired an increasingly abstract meaning. Originally this word denoted political co-authority of subjects and rulers in the state, as a form of communal bond. It became a term that is currently used in the life of

297

the church, marriage and family life, in school and university, business life and sport. This concept is now taken to be synonymous with other concepts which do not stem from the sphere of the state but from the sphere of family life, for example, or from the sphere of factory labour. Various terms can now be used inter-changeably: democracy, maturity, partnership, equality, co-authority, co-responsibility, humanitarianism, etc.

This vague language, and its abstraction from different realms, implies a danger. Imperceptibly, the life patterns of one community might begin to serve as normative for another. This occurs at the expense of the unfolding of a community's character or nature. Thus, for example, the pastoral writing of the Dutch Reformed Church on the political responsibility of the church reflects a conspicuous foundation of political democracy. The argument suggests that:

> . . . the *church* acknowledges a relation between God and man, in which man is not struck dumb when confronted with the Word of God, but speaks, judges, wills and acts *with* God. The relation of God and man . . . does not only mean a form of dependence but also a form of voluntary subordination, by which the authorities are recognised as such and offer forms of co-responsibility to those over whom they have been placed.

Here the leading thought of democracy lies in the consideration that man ought to be – or should become – of age. Therefore, as a free citizen of the state, he ought to participate as co-determinator in public life. Such an idea is based on the premise that each person should be a mature member of the church. This relation between God and man, visible in the proper experience of church membership, must also realise itself in the state.

In this train of thought we can glimpse the deepest foundation of political democracy – the way in which God has ordained His relation to man. We would not like to suggest that the situation in the church (man's relation to God) must therefore be the same in the state and other communities.

On the contrary, democracy ought to be like this everywhere; it must be like this in the church and everywhere in life *in a typical way*. But the way we experience democracy in the church does not have to become the norm for the way in which it is realised in other communities. The differences in the formulation of the problem depends on whether the nature-grace scheme, as it takes a Protestant shape in the Lutheran doctrine of the two domains, has been banned.

Authority and Co-Authority

In the creation-order, God has spoken his "Word." He called and still calls all things into existence and continues their existence. Therefore, the creatures are what they are, and man is what he is: a creature called to answer. His life is a response to the Word of God as Creator and Redeemer. In the creational order which forms the human answer-structure, God has revealed His will as norm-beginning (principle). From God's side, the creational order is the creational start. It is the dynamic stimulus and religious guide that makes human life possible, gives it its contents and directs us to the perspectival centre and integration point in Jesus Christ.

Concerning human life, *the creational start* – the creational Word of God which calls life into existence – is a manifestation of the will of God, whereby He calls man to co-authority and gives him room to accept this responsibility. God provides norms for human life by giving it initially a beginning/ principle which must be continued and made concrete. The responding-character of human life in thought and action implies that man, in answer to and in continuation of this normative beginning, continues by giving norms and forms to life. Man is God's image, and being His image, he is also God's collaborator in the crystallisation of the creation and in the realisation and unfolding of life. God's creative start retains its validity. There is no room in this view of man and life for a personalistic, structureless realisation of life.

In the creative order God sets out the trail on which man must work. He draws the dotted lines that man must complete as creator under the authority of and in imitation of the Creator. As God's image, he is

God's collaborator in the maintenance and unfolding of the creation "in-the-beginning." In this way man has co-authority; he is king under God. God's authority calls man to co-authority, to co-legislation. God's work as creator made man his own image: co-creator, co-legislator, and co-worker, under and after God, in the footsteps of God and walking in the direction of His purpose.

The *dynamic stimulus* implies the creational order and the human answer-structure given in this situation. God did not retreat after the start of creation. God remains present and continuously asserts His creator's will with all His might. He is the originator for all life, so it cannot stagnate. There is progression in creation through the continuous dynamics of God's presence, in which man maintains his creator's will. The old idea of the collaboration of God as an element in God's providence was not altogether wrong, but merely a reversal of the proper order: man does not work while God collaborates. The opposite is true: God works and man collaborates, whether inside or outside the boundaries of the order of creation set out by God. Man moves in the direction that God points out – toward salvation or away from salvation.

The religious direction is also given to human life by the order of creation. In and through the order of creation, each aspect of human life refers to the final encompassing questions of the meaning of life, or origin and purpose. The questions can only be answered in faith, and in them *Christian* faith in its contents and direction are determined by God's revelation. God's Word-revelation in Holy Scriptures shows us the way because it shows us Christ, the Redeemer of creation. He brings man back into the community of the covenant with the Creator and restores life by placing him anew on the "paths of righteousness," on the "way of life." Through His Spirit, He leads us in all truth and guides us to true reality.

Particular Co-Authority

This is a biblical thought that is common today. It is fully expressed in the rhymed Dutch version of the Lord's Prayer in these lines: "Dat elk als kind aan uw gelijk," and "in zijn doen uw beeltnis blijk" ("That everyone as child, equal to you" and "in his doing your image appears"). The sovereign Creator made man in this fashion. With His divine authority as Creator, He calls man to the realisation of his Creator's will, of which He gave the principles and foundation in the creational order.

In the philosophical theory of structure, this Christian view of life reflects a richly varied image of the diversity of life. We are able to observe different and particular kinds of authority, whereby individuals may have a say over others in diverse community relations. In the Christian view of life, man rightly acknowledges that authority in diverse "human ordinances" has its origin in the divine authority over man. It "pleases God to rule us through their hands," suggests a well-known phrase from the Catechism of

Heidelberg.

In these relations of authority, man is the image of God, individually and in the community. In the practice of authority, leaders may be "followers of God." And herein lies the deepest Christian criticism of the deterioration of authority in human relations. Christians decry the dictatorial absolutism of authority and the disappearance of authority in the name of solidarity, equality and "Partnerschaft." Nor do they accept the humanistic, pragmatic view of authority as a practical necessity, founded in the majority will of a collectivity.

In being God's image and collaborator – which is the fundamental situation of human life – we discover the co-authority in relations of authority. The initial or *a priori* character of God's order of creation calls man, under God's *guidance* and in God's footsteps, to unfold life toward the normative side. However, this very trail, given in the order of creation, shows us at the same time a great variety of ways in which man may be God's collaborator in giving norms and forms to life.

The normative structure of social situations does not allow the same practices everywhere. The relations of authority and co-authority in marriage, family, school, church, university, trade, state, association are always structurally different. Hence, the concrete forms and figures in which these relations are realised will also be different. To nullify these differences would be an impoverishment of life. Instead, a

303

comparison of one structure with another will be an inspiration to the improvement of form. This happens continually. These changes of form, which are historically modified, are not voluntary and purely subjective changes – unless they are detrimental to the particular sector of life. The normative structure of a particular community remains the primary principle for the evolution of life and gives direction to a dynamic and progressive development.

Social Responsibility

The diversity and particular character of human life derives its inner coherence, deep unity and only origin from the divine Creator's will. Man's survival after the fall can be ascribed to the divine, sustaining, and redeeming work. Therefore, human life, in its diverse *social* connections, remains connected to the Creator's and Redeemer's Word. Social life manifests itself as a *collective* or *communal* experience of human responsibility. Guidance of authority in every social community implies a *primary* responsibility. But according to the nature of the community authority (office), exclusive and sole responsibility of functionaries or authorities is impossible. It is not the authority they derive from their own creation or power; nor is sole responsibility a creation or function of a collectivity. All authority comes from God. In the experience of the relations of authority and subordination, both the individuals and the community have to behave as God's image and collaborator.

In addition to the normative structures in the

order of creation, there is a social responsibility toward God. Once again, this responsibility to God is no different from the responsibility toward our fellow-man. The latter is included in the encompassing realm of the religious ground-situation of social life.

The Scheme: Means-End

It was Aristotle in particular who, in the spirit of Western thinking, introduced the theoretical scheme "means/end." In the future, people may realise one of the most influential changes effected by the philosophy of the Cosmonomic Idea. In the realm of social ethics, the *priority* of the means/end scheme (taken over early in Christian thought without any criticism) was replaced by a more important issue: what is the divine law for each sector of human life? It is a case of seeking God's will, revealed in the order of creation, in which the Word revelation entered. Afterward, the question about concrete ends and means can only be asked within the normative structural realm of a social community. In this train of thought, "man" or the harmonious unfolding of his personality or "the community" can never be an end in itself. Human responsibility, as well as social responsibility, is fundamentally related to God's creation and His redeeming Word. Based on these premises, man responds to God individually and in his social relations, with his concrete life.

Particular Co-Responsibility

In the natural, collective realisation of life in a special

305

sector, and on the basis of the divine structural law created for it, every individual member of a group or community is *co*-responsible for the collective answer which God claims from us. There exists, therefore, a close connection between, for example, co-responsibility and co-authority. The total answer (concrete life in a social context) manifests itself, for example, in the relations of authority and sub-ordination. It is therefore correct to say, *in general*, that co-responsibility for a particular part of life also implies co-authority. Nevertheless, subordination is not discontinued, because human authority has to orient itself to the way in which God exerts His authority.

Specific and typical situations of concrete life compel us to ask one question again and again. Are co-responsibility and co-authority adapted to the normative structure of the typical situation? This historical law of the labour-and-function division co-determines the extent of particular co-responsibility. No overall functional theory can be offered, nor can a universal model be derived from one particular social structure. Here the related special sciences must offer us more clarity in the historically variable, but still typical, structures of each social community.

CHAPTER 14

Freedom

Necessary Philosophical Orientation

SINCE ANCIENT TIMES the idea of freedom has fascinated mankind. In the realms of philosophy and theology, publications on freedom are endless. And during the last few centuries, freedom has figured prominently in sociology, psychology, and other "human and social sciences," including "ethics." In fact, a philosophy of freedom reflects on the orientation-schemes, points of reference, thought categories and even the point of departure of scientific thought.

Freedom and Origin

In my opinion, the phenomenon of freedom can only be treated properly from the perspective of the created *origin* of all the phenomena in human life. The origin, root and central source of human freedom is found in their original existence. Only from the standpoint of the radical unity of all diversity in our existence can we survey the diversity of what we call freedom.

Historical and Etymological Approach

It may be useful to look at the origin of the *concept* of freedom, in so far as this has been traced by experts. Some claim we must go back in literature as far as possible to see what the notion of freedom meant to the Greeks and other old cultures. Eventually we will see how the meaning changes through history to become what we understand of it today. Thus, for example, H. Schlier in the great Lexicon of Kittle on New Testament Greek sees a great constancy of meaning throughout the ages. According to his research, the Greeks already thought freedom implied being one's own master, determining one's own future, being independent, etc.

In contrast, we have the method of Muller in his book *Freedom in the Ancient World.* He does not follow the lead of etymology or semantics but starts off with his own view of freedom. In his *a priori* definition, freedom is "the condition of being able to choose and to carry out purposes." Using this criterion, he determines where and how freedom existed in the past. (We will omit this issue from our discussion here because it belongs to the realms of science-theory.)

Etymological Examination of D. Nestlé

We need not over-estimate the value of etymological studies in order to see their practical value. The science of etymology tries to combat the decay of language, which manifests itself in the arbitrary use of word-sounds. Etymology can serve as a kind of conscience for linguistics, not as the final arbiter of contradictions, but surely as a reliable guide.

Summary of Nestlé's Investigation

The Indo-Germanic word "vrij" existed as an adjective long before the abstract concept "freedom" was a noun, and before the substantive free(man) – Dutch "vrije" – was in use. The contradiction between free man and slave comes to the surface quite later. According to Nestlé, the contradiction free-unfree (in the sense of bondage) is not original.

From the start, the Greek languages and the West-Germanic languages (which all belong to Indo-Germanic) used "free" as an adjective, meaning "belonging to friends and relatives." Hence the secondary meaning of love ("lief"). In Germanic the word is "frija" (which is related to "frijo" woman) – Dutch "vrouw;" hence our word love-making ("vrijen").

The Greek word for free is "eleuteros," the Latin is "liber," which in the singular form means "free" and in the plural also "children." Both the Greek elutheros and the Latin liber go back to the same stem, "leudh," which (in the Germanic languages) results in the words "Leute" and "luiden" (people). But these are words that in diverse Germanic and Slavonic languages (including Frisian and Russian) stem from the word "luid" or "ljud," which means people or national community. The often-used Frisian name for a boy – "Ljudger" – means something like leader of the people, the man who really belongs there.

In general, Nestlé comes to the conclusion that the communal basic meaning of all words for *free* (vrij) in different languages is: *the concrete life in one's own (primitive) social milieu.* Someone who is *at home*, in his Heim, his Heimat, someone who does not dwell in foreign lands and does not feel un-heim-isch, is free. The original question is not: who is free? The question is: where is man free? The answer is that a man is free at home, in his clan, in his family, in his polis (city-state) and among his own fellows ("luidges").

Following the time of the Greeks, the word "free" was set in contrast by particular situations. First there is the contrast-relation with those who are not present with the person or who does not belong there. Whoever is *present* but does not belong there is either a *guest*, a *stranger,* or a *slave.* Guests and strangers are not, by definition, free men. A slave is not unfree because of his bondage, submissiveness, or subjecting, but because he is *strange* and of foreign origin. He is un-heimisch – not at home with his own people.

In Greece during the 8th century B.C., we do not find in the poems of Homeros any contrast between free and unfree people; we only find the adjective free. The current interpretation that Homeros already knew slavery is countered by Nestlé. It is not the commissioned labour that makes the kidnapped woman Andromache so miserable, but her labour *there*, in a foreign land, far from her city, her family,

310

her home.

In the 7th and 6th century, during the great crisis of the culture of ancient Greece, a radical change manifested itself. The patrician noble families, who were agrarians, were outranked by the new aristocracy of the tradesmen. A differentiation process now manifested itself thoroughly in society. As cities emerged, the poor and the rich, the slaves and the free men, were distinguished. Nobility and ordinary people stood opposite each other. *Solon*, one of the "seven wise men," managed to avoid a crisis in the Athens of the 6th century by giving society a revolutionary new structure. He forced the people to accept a new compromise: the slaves were bought free by money from the public treasury, and judicature was reorganised to limit the right of the nobility. On an economical basis the people were now divided into four classes.

In this period the concept "Polis" (city, state) was connected to the idea of the community of free men. The contrast to the unfree men, the slaves, is new, but is as yet not accentuated. The emphasis to a great extent still lies on the original meaning of being free — being home, in the familiar sphere. The term does not distinguish the being-free of the citizens, but the being-citizen of the free men. Solon does not preach freedom but rather the polis, the political community, the city of the fathers, the motherland, the places where the gods give prosperous life. *There* man comes to real humanity; there he really is a political citizen.

311

Mother earth is also free only if she becomes a city, the city of Solon, with justice and order.

Conclusion

Both etymologically and semantically, human freedom did not originally stand in opposition to a certain bondage. On the contrary, freedom meant functioning in the community, *first* in the primitive home-community and family-community (kingship) – and later in the political community. This was a *fundamental condition* for being free – at least, in an historical perspective! In terms of the use of the word "free," man was placed opposite a stranger, then later opposite a slave.

The Need to Orientate the Idea of Freedom to Social Relations, Special Science and Philosophy

Although an historical and linguistic approach to the idea of freedom is interesting and valuable, the meaning of the term is limited by the very porous boundaries of these special sciences. In philosophical ethics it is important to explicate the *philosophical* quality of freedom (which usually is not unfolded). Therefore, we must remember that even the semantic restriction of meaning must be focussed on the use of the word freedom in *diverse social relations*. This calls for a more precise social-philosophical circumscription of relations in the whole of society.

Freedom Is Concrete Freedom

Philosophically it makes little sense to meditate on the notion "freedom." *Concrete freedom is always a freedom in a particular way*. The same holds true for "lack of freedom." In the realm of science, which so often encounters errors in the labyrinth of "Allgemeinsbegriffe," we should ask one primary question: in what sense does freedom exist? But for such a question to make sense, we need a ground plan of the possibilities-of-being-meaning, a point of reference, a table of categories, an overview.

The insight into the nine normative aspects offers a unique perspective for looking at the different possibilities of freedom. We should also consider how one specific aspect can qualify different types of social structures. We realise that economic freedom is different from freedom of faith, and freedom of faith is not the same as freedom of religion (i.e., organised freedom of cult). We also experience freedom of organisation (power-formation) and of the press (expression of opinion), by which we can set foot in the domain of political (i.e., pertaining to public law) liberties. In this way every social structure has its own liberties which are qualified by the structure of the community in question. In the statutes, fundamentals, regulations, etc., the liberties in such a community are qualified and thereby limited. Whoever does not abide by them cannot be tolerated as a member of the organisation or community.

Within the limits of a concrete societal structure

there is scope for individual experience of freedom. The scope is different everywhere, and its extent depends wholly on the nature (structure) of the community in question and its internal regulations.

Another problem we encounter is freedom in the mutual relations between diverse social structures. But this is a typical social-philosophical problem.

Freedom and Law

In general, we recognise that "absolute freedom" does not exist; freedom is always freedom-in-bondage. The importance of this recognition depends on how we evaluate this relation philosophically. Is this bondage a necessary evil? Are freedom and bondage essentially each other's opposite or rivals? Or are they complementary ideas? All of these suggestions have been advocated at various times. For each definition, proverbs were invented (e.g., "real freedom abides by the laws").

The struggle to define "real" freedom is, in fact, as old as humanity. Even in the Bible we detect a difference of opinion on the subject of freedom during those times. Jesus also spoke of being "really free" in opposition to pseudo-freedom.

On a personal note, I was once welcomed to East Berlin – the "really free part of Berlin." The differences here do not only concern the dilemma of freedom/captivity; *in* this dilemma we also confront an idea of what *real* freedom is. What one person calls freedom will be slavery to another. The East

German considers himself to be really free, but the West European questions why he is not allowed to visit his family in Western Berlin and has no freedom of speech, etc. Both persons consider public law as a *sine qua non* for freedom. Laws must be righteous to guarantee freedom. But which laws are righteous and which laws guarantee freedom?

Political freedom, for example, is related to cultural freedom. The American ideal to change young African States into Western democracies is, in my opinion, misguided. The African people still need the cultural freedom that Western Europe struggled to obtain. It took Europe close to 2000 years to attain such freedom.

Freedom can be investigated from two viewpoints – a modal and a structural one. A modal investigation concerns examples like freedom of movement, economic freedom, and linguistic freedom (the freedom to express yourself in more than one language).

Structural freedom has to do with political freedom, freedom of religion, etc. An employee is bound by the regulations of his firm, but his employer does not prescribe membership in a certain church. He has freedom of religion. Whether the employee is married or behaves himself morally in private life, etc., is no concern of his employer.

However, being a member of a certain church will limit a person's freedom. He is not free to believe and do what he likes. Ecclesiastical freedom differs

315

from political freedom, a point that was not always recognised. The famous decision on freedom of religion of Augsburg in 1575 forced the people to choose the same religion as the king. The alternative was exile or imprisonment.

In the view of these facts, the definition cited above – freedom is the condition of being able to choose and to carry out purposes – begins to show its limitations.

Which are righteous laws, guaranteeing freedom? God's law is truly a law of freedom. Freedom in the different domains of societal life must be oriented to the structural principles of normative creational order. The rules of family life must serve moral love and trust between parents and children. Laws pertaining to family life have no validity outside that sphere. Freedom in that state, meanwhile, requires righteous laws for *public* life. The freedom of non-stately spheres (business, church, family, sport, science) must never be impaired by public laws.

Freedom in the Central—Religious Sense or in the Modally Qualified Sense

Let us briefly pursue the subject of freedom and origin once more. We realise that a philosophical-praxiological discussion on freedom only becomes meaningful when we consciously make use of an orientation-scheme (we do so in an unconscious manner regardless). We borrow the criterion for our approach to the problem of freedom from our main anthropological distinction. This concerns the differentiation between the *central* meaningfulness and the modal meaning diversity in the freedom, without making this distinction into a *dissociation*! (Here we recall the distinction between modal aspects of reality and structures of concrete phenomena.)

Thus we understand the real freedom in a central-religious sense as a "freedom-in-Christ," who is the root and source of every other actual freedom. All diversity of meaning that freedom can have in the transitory human existence, and in which all distinctions must be made, has its central meaningfulness in transcending "person-centre," the "heart" or "I" of man.

Freedom from, Freedom to, Freedom in

If we consult numerous lexicons and dictionaries on the word "freedom," we come across the distinction "freedom to" and "freedom from," also called positive and negative freedom. The premise is that human liberty is something like freedom-of-choice, where man is "free" to choose a certain aim. This distinction surely has some merit, but not much. It only becomes relevant on the basis of an insight into the relation of freedom and bondage.

But the meaningfulness of real freedom *transcends all concrete positive or negative freedom.* The meaningfulness of this freedom exists in only *one* expression, which surpasses all practical and theoretical comprehension. I refer to the unique usage in the Bible, namely the *freedom-in-Christ.*

317

The "Law-of-Freedom"

According to biblical insight, we were created to be free, and we are consistently "called to freedom." This the Bible calls the "law of freedom." An expression like this can only be understood when we see man in his threefold central relation: to himself, to his fellow-man, and to God. God's "law" is the possibility, the vocation, and the motivation of all types of freedom. If we distinguish the law-side, we can say that *freedom in every sense is the situation in conformity to the law*. Naturally this is a very general and abstract formulation. But surely it is a fundamental and philosophical distinction in the sense of *thought directed from and to the origin*.

It is valid also in the case of the more concrete consideration of aspects and social structures. But a lot more must be taken into consideration each time. Here we land in the territory of social philosophy and of the special sciences. Freedom must not be considered as something formal without contents; it is a certain quality of life, measured by the life-law valid for it. Freedom is what corresponds to the law of life. This is the very starting point for a scientific and practical discussion. We can then ask a specific question. What are the implications of the life-law in the diverse aspects and structures? In this way we limit any unqualified talk about "freedom-of-choice" to the different structures of these social communities in which the specific liberties can be determined in more detail.

318

Freedom in the Bible (John 8:30-36)

"Jesus said to those Jews which had believed in him . . . ye shall know the truth and the truth shall make you free." The disciples understood this promise in a *political* sense. They thought of freedom as the opposite of slavery. But then Jesus told them: "If the Son shall make you free, ye shall be free *indeed*."

Obviously, Jesus uses the term "free" in different senses. He puts freedom from slavery over against being free indeed. Does this mean that freedom from slavery is not real freedom? Or that liberation from slavery is not overly important? We know better. The whole history of the Old Testament people of the covenant describes the repeated surrender of the Israelites into enemy slavery as a form of punishment. According to the Bible, freedom from slavery in a political sense is very important. But taken in a central-religious sense we must state that a slave can be free, and an oppressed church can be free.

Freedom in Christ must never be separated from the experience of freedom in the various domains of life. On the contrary, freedom in Christ is the religious root of our whole Christian life. It becomes a reality in all the spheres of life according to the typical structural norms of each sphere, given as a creational ordinance. The inspiration for our differentiated freedom comes from the central all-encompassing freedom in Christ.

Freedom in Principle

We are never free in the full sense of the word. Christ set us free, but the fulfillment of our freedom is something we expect only with the second coming of Christ and thereafter. In the practical language of faith, a Christian can confess: I am free, I was liberated by Christ, in Him I am a free man. In theological terms we can make a similar confession. Our freedom is a freedom in principle . . . in this temporal life.

Scripture Index

Subject Index

327

T